KT-447-407

choosing the right wine
beverley blanning

For UK order enquiries: please contact Bookpoint Ltd, 130 Milton Park, Abingdon, Oxon OX14 4SB. Telephone: +44 (0) 1235 827720. Fax: +44 (0) 1235 400454. Lines are open 09.00–17.00, Monday to Saturday, with a 24-hour message answering service. Details about our titles and how to order are available at www.teachyourself.co.uk

For USA order enquiries: please contact McGraw-Hill Customer Services, PO Box 545, Blacklick, OH 43004-0545, USA. Telephone: 1-800-722-4726. Fax: 1-614-755-5645.

For Canada order enquiries: please contact McGraw-Hill Ryerson Ltd, 300 Water St, Whitby, Ontario L1N 9B6, Canada. Telephone: 905 430 5000. Fax: 905 430 5020.

Long renowned as the authoritative source for self-guided learning – with more than 50 million copies sold worldwide – the **teach yourself** series includes over 500 titles in the fields of languages, crafts, hobbies, business, computing and education.

British Library Cataloguing in Publication Data: a catalogue record for this title is available from the British Library.

Library of Congress Catalog Card Number: on file.

First published in UK 2008 by Hodder Education, part of Hachette Livre UK, 338 Euston Road, London, NW1 3BH.

First published in US 2008 by The McGraw-Hill Companies, Inc.

This edition published 2008.

The **teach yourself** name is a registered trade mark of Hodder Headline.

Typeset by Transet Ltd, Coventry.
Printed in Great Britain for Hodder Education, an Hachette Livre UK Company, 338 Euston Road, London NW1 3BH, by CPI Cox & Wyman, Reading, Berkshire, RG1 8EX.

The publisher has used its best endeavours to ensure that the URLs for external websites referred to in this book are correct and active at the time of going to press. However, the publisher and the author have no responsibility for the websites and can make no guarantee that a site will remain live or that the content will remain relevant, decent or appropriate.

Hachette Livre UK's policy is to use papers that are natural, renewable and recyclable products and made from wood grown in sustainable forests. The logging and manufacturing processes are expected to conform to the environmental regulations of the country of origin.

Impression number   10 9 8 7 6 5 4 3 2 1
Year   2012 2011 2010 2009 2008

iii

contents

For my father, who taught himself.

acknowledgements

The views expressed in this book are mine. Wine is, and always should be, a personal choice; my aim here has been to provide the tools to make choosing wine stress-free, and to give an overview of the most interesting wines that are readily available to buy. There are many more worthy wines in the world than space allows coverage for here, but I hope that you will find enough in these pages to inspire you to follow your own taste to discover new and exciting wines to enjoy.

This book has benefited from the eyes and wisdom of friends and colleagues. Particular thanks are due to Tim Hanni MW and Mark de Vere MW for their time and insights on food and wine. I also appreciate the assistance of Nichola Bellini, Angie Forer, Marina Gayan MW, Julia Harding MW, John Hoskins MW, Harriet Inglis, Dr Greg Jones, Margaret Rand, Jancis Robinson MW OBE, Jean-Michel Valette MW, Monty Waldin and Guy Woodward. I am grateful for the patience and support of all of my family, especially Geoff, Leo and Oscar.

Beverley Blanning MW
September 2008

introduction

Do you like wine, but wish you knew more about how to choose it? Do you panic if someone hands you the wine list in a restaurant? Have you ever tasted a delicious wine, but never managed to remember the name of it, or find anything similar again? Or do you think all wine tastes the same, and wonder what all the fuss is about? If you are at all curious about wine, this book has the answers you need.

Selecting wine can instil irrational fear into the most sensible person. There are so many wines to choose from, many of which are labelled in incomprehensible foreign languages. Even if you are fortunate enough to find a description on the back label of a bottle, you still don't know if you – or the person you are buying it for – will like it. There is also the worry of somehow looking silly or less well-informed than you feel you should be in front of someone who knows more about wine than you do.

Wine *can* be a complicated subject, but don't let this put you off. It is this wonderful diversity that makes it such a pleasure to discover, and the good news is that a little knowledge goes a long way. Wine is also remarkably easily self-taught, and is the most sociable of pastimes to explore with a group of friends.

Using the simple techniques explained in this book, you will enjoy wine more from the very start. In the following chapters you will find practical examples of readily available wines to try and advice on how to taste that will enable you to choose wine with confidence every time. You will learn why wine tastes the way it does, and – most importantly – learn to identify your own preferences, which are as individual as you are. And as you taste and compare more wines, you will soon be able to distinguish one style of wine from another and easily pick the right wine for any occasion.

Learning about wine will open the door to a world of diversity and enjoyment unmatched by any other type of food or drink. Wine is one of the most enduring and sociable of life's pleasures. You have nothing to fear and everything to gain from learning a little more about this wonderful gift of nature.

A word about wine snobs, show-offs and bores

We've all met these people. Their behaviour could put you off wine for life. Please try to ignore them, or better still, avoid them altogether. If what matters to you most is the status of the name on the bottle, or how much you can impress by the price you paid, this is not the book for you – although you will find advice in these pages about which wines to serve to hold your own against such people. I've never met a true wine lover who fell into one of these categories. Certainly, there are a few wine geeks about (including, I confess, your author). You may even become one yourself by the end of this book. But learning about wine should not turn you into a bore or a snob. When you truly discover and learn, the need for pretence becomes irrelevant.

... and a word about prices

If you are fairly new to buying wine, the range of prices can be as bewildering as the choice. Faced with a selection of unknown bottles, it can be tempting to shop according to price. Why is there so much difference in the price of wines? And to what extent does price really reflect quality? If a £4 bottle tastes good enough, why pay more?

Well, there are a couple of very good reasons to spend a little more on a bottle of wine. The first is tax. A significant, fixed amount is added to the cost of every bottle. If you are shopping in the UK, the excise duty on a bottle of wine is now £1.46 (and £1.87 on any sparkling wine). This is added to the cost of the wine before the calculation of VAT. This means that if you buy a £4 bottle of wine, more than half of this price is tax. The remaining £1.94 needs to cover the cost of the bottle, and a margin for the local retailer, which leaves precious little for the liquid. Do the same calculation for an £8 wine, and it's clear that the value of the wine is much higher – so you are getting a lot more wine for your money. This is not to say there are no good wines at £4, or that all expensive wines are necessarily good. But it is true that there are many more interesting wines to choose from if you are prepared to venture above the basic price levels.

Some people are reluctant to pay more for a bottle of wine because they feel they won't be able to tell the difference, so it is a waste of money to do so. There are two responses to this. First, it has been shown time and again that if you give anyone two wines, they will probably prefer the 'better' wine. Second, it really depends what you are looking for from wine. If you have a single wine you like and have no curiosity to try anything else, you should probably stick with it (and maybe put this book back on the shelf). But if you do this, you are missing out on all the fun of wine. This is a drink that can be enjoyed at any level, but the more you know, the more you'll want to explore. By understanding why you like the wines you do, you'll be able to branch out and discover new styles of wines you'll also love. The pleasures of wine can be appreciated by anyone who is prepared to invest a little time and money in the subject.

part one

where to begin

01

getting started

In this chapter you will learn:
- why anyone can learn about wine
- where to find answers to your questions in this book.

Initial questions

Before you get started tasting wine, this chapter addresses some of the initial questions you might have.

What is wine?

Wine is nothing more complicated than fermented grape juice. If you crush grapes and add yeast, you can make wine. Wine includes all shades of red, white and rosé, Champagne and other fizzy wines, sherry, port, Madeira and other fortified wines. It does not include spirits or, for the purposes of this book, wines made from fruit other than grapes. See Chapter 05 for more details on how the way a wine is made influences its taste.

If it's so simple, why are there so many different wines?

Even though wine is the product of a single fruit, the grape, there are many different varieties of grape, which all have individual flavours (see Chapter 03). The place the grapes are grown affects their flavour, as does the hand and creativity of the person who makes the wine (this is explained in Chapters 04 and 05). And as consumers, we all have different tastes (see Chapter 06 for how to understand your own taste), and most of us enjoy variety, so there are many different styles of wine produced to cater for this (see Chapter 07 for how to identify wine styles).

Can anyone learn to taste wine?

Anyone who can taste food can taste wine. See Chapter 02 for a simple, step-by-step guide to tasting wine and which wines to start out with.

Why do I need to know about grapes?

There are many thousands of grape varieties used to make wine. You don't need to know them all, but if you know about the main varieties used, you'll immediately have an understanding for the likely taste of the wine from the grape variety on the label of the bottle. Each variety has its own distinct character, and this will determine the kind of wine it is likely to produce. Grape varieties differ in terms of flavour profiles, and also in terms of their physical structure. Some will have thicker skins than others; some will be sweeter and some more acidic; some will taste of flowers, others of blackcurrants or plums, tobacco, herbs or spices, or many other flavours. Some grape varieties may have such a strong character that they need no other supporting flavours and will frequently be used to make single varietal wines, while others are better suited to be combined in blends with complementary varieties (see box below). You'll learn more about the different types of grapes and the wines they make in Chapters 02 and 03.

Try these

Compare a glass each of these two white wines to see the difference between a wine made from a single grape variety and one made from a blend of two varieties:

- Sauvignon Blanc from South Africa, Chile or New Zealand
- Sémillon/Chardonnay blend from South Eastern Australia.

Notice the strong character of the Sauvignon Blanc compared to the blend. Its powerful smell and flavours come solely from the character of the Sauvignon Blanc grape variety, not from any added flavours. This is the reason Sauvignon Blanc is usually not blended with other grape varieties. Sémillon and Chardonnay are grape varieties that are often blended with other varieties to make more interesting wines.

How long does it take to learn how to choose the right wine?

You could spend the rest of your life studying wine and still not know everything. But you can learn the basics of how to taste wine in just a few minutes. Once you have this skill, you can taste and compare different wines in a whole new light. The great thing about wine is that every little thing you learn you can apply right away. So you can make better choices in your purchases from the start.

Is the name of the wine's grape variety always on the bottle?

Unfortunately, no. In new world wine-producing countries (such as the USA, Australia, South Africa and Chile) the grape variety is almost always on the label. But in the traditional wine growing regions of Europe, there is often no clue about the grape variety or varieties on the bottle. This is particularly true of the more famous regions (Bordeaux, Burgundy, Tuscany, Rioja and so on) where the name of the place has always been thought to be a better indicator of the style of the wine than the grape varieties used to make it. This is not very helpful for a person starting to learn about wine. See Chapter 03 for a guide to knowing what grape varieties you can expect to find in wines that give no clues on the label, and Chapters 08 and 09 to learn about wine styles by region.

Why are some wines more expensive than others?

The price of a wine reflects the price of growing the grapes and making the wine, and its demand relative to the quantity available. Price will reflect local costs (it is far cheaper to harvest grapes by hand in Argentina than it is in France, for example) and the scale of production. Many expensive wines are made in tiny quantities, where economies of scale are not possible. Some of the best wines are made from grapes grown on steep slopes, or on difficult terrain that is costly to work, but that yields the best quality grapes, and this is reflected in the price.

I only like white wine (or rosé, or red) – is there any point in learning about anything else?

Yes. If you understand why you like the wine you know you like, you can apply this knowledge to choose other wines (and probably of all colours) that will appeal to you as well. You'll probably be inclined to explore beyond your current boundaries and widen the range of wines you'll enjoy.

Is Champagne wine?

Yes, Champagne starts out as a normal, rather tart, wine and then undergoes a lengthy process of a second fermentation and storage in bottle to make it sparkle.

What does 'vintage' mean?

Vintage is simply the term used to describe the year the wine was made. Wine from the 2008 vintage was made from grapes harvested in the autumn of 2008 in the northern hemisphere, and the spring of 2008 in the southern hemisphere. The reason the vintage is noted on the bottle is because the weather conditions during the year will have a significant impact on the quality of the wine produced. It also tells you how old the wine is.

Where does the colour come from in red wine?

Red wines get their colour from the skins of the grapes. Grapes with thick, dark skins will produce wines with the deepest colour. The pulp is not a source of colour in wine, except in one or two rare instances.

How is rosé wine made?

Rosé wine is made using the same fermentation process as that of red or white wine. The usual way to make rosé is to use black grapes that have been crushed and soaked for a short time with the dark skins in contact with the grape juice. This imparts the pink colour. Rarely (but more commonly in Champagne), red wine and white wine can be mixed together to make rosé wine.

What about organic wine?

Organic practice is a growing trend in wine, as everyone tries to be more sustainable. But to be a green wine shopper there are other things to think about as well as the way the grapes are grown. Read Chapter 13 to find out more about how to be more sustainable in your wine shopping.

How can I choose the right wine for every occasion and every type of food?

There is no 'right' wine for any individual occasion or dish. There are many wines to suit different occasions and types of food. This book will tell you how to choose the right wine for *you*. See Chapter 10 to discover how to match the wine you like with the food you like.

How will I know if a wine is good or bad?

There are few absolutes in wine, and your personal judgement is the most valuable tool you have to evaluate a wine. If you don't like it, it's probably not good – and vice versa. See Chapter 13 for how to identify the main faults you are likely to come across when buying wine in a restaurant. Most wine is made to be drunk as soon as it is bottled, so if it's not to your taste, you can use your tasting techniques to work out why you don't like it and then move on to something else. However, some wines are made to be aged and to improve over time. These might start out tasting unpalatable, but end up delicious. With practice, you'll soon learn how to identify if a wine is balanced (see Chapter 02), whether it has potential to improve and which styles of wines you like the best.

How can I tell if a wine is sweet or dry before I buy it?

Unfortunately, you can't always tell. But there are usually enough clues on the bottle for you to be able to work it out. See Chapter 07 to learn about different wine styles, Chapters 08 and 09 to learn about the kinds of wine you'll expect to find in different parts of the world, and Chapter 12 for advice on deciphering wine labels.

Is Riesling always sweet and nasty?

No. There is plenty of dry and delicious Riesling wine from Australia and Alsace – and even Germany, where the Riesling produced is now mostly dry. There are also many high-quality sweet Rieslings (especially from Germany) that bear no resemblence to the bad stuff.

Can I serve red wine chilled?

Yes. Most lighter reds taste good slightly chilled (especially when the weather is hot, because they quickly warm up once poured), but don't be afraid to cool down other reds slightly to freshen them up a little. See Chapter 11 for more advice on serving temperatures for different styles of wine.

How long can I keep a wine after opening the bottle?

It depends on the wine and the techniques you use to preserve it. Most wine can be kept a few days after opening if it is stored properly. See Chapter 14 for more on this.

Do I need to buy any special equipment to learn about wine?

No, although you will want to use glasses that slope inwards at the rim because you will be able to smell and taste a lot more in your wine (see Chapter 02). Once you start using glasses like these, you'll find it hard to go back to an open or V-shaped glass.

Is it going to be expensive to buy all these wines?

Wine tends to be as expensive as you want to make it. For comparative tastings, it's a good idea to taste with a few friends to share the cost – and also to share your experiences. There are many, many delicious wines that don't cost the earth. But there are very few very cheap wines that are really interesting to taste. As you begin to explore, you will find you get more value by spending a little more. And once you are more confident about which wines you know you'll like, it will be less of a risk to splash out occasionally on something special.

How can I avoid making a fool of myself?

Don't be afraid to ask questions. The only people who will think you a fool for not knowing about wine are people who really don't know much themselves. Anyone who does know about wine – a sommelier in a restaurant, an assistant in a wine shop, or a friend you trust – will be very happy to share that knowledge with you. Try it – you'll be surprised at just how passionate keen wine lovers are about their subject.

Doesn't learning about wine take away all the fun?

Not at all – although if you are the kind of person who likes to talk about the wine you are tasting throughout dinner, you'd better find yourself some like-minded drinking companions.

Is there a shortcut to learning about wine?

There are plenty of shortcuts and tips to speed up your learning about wine within the covers of this book. The fastest way to learn, though, is to taste as many different wines as you can, and to observe carefully what you taste. Tasting with friends is a good way to see alternative points of view and helps to define your own taste.

Why do the labels on the bottles have to be so complicated?

Sometimes there are good reasons for labels to be complicated, but most of the time it is nothing but a chore for the person choosing the wine. Wines from some parts of the world will always have complicated and unfamiliar labels (Germany and Burgundy come to mind), while others will always be refreshingly simple: Australia and the USA, for example. See Chapter 12 for advice on understanding wine labels.

Aren't screwcaps just for cheap wine?

No. Screwcaps are increasingly being used on very good wines, especially white wines. They keep wine fresh and unaffected by wine faults.

How can I tell if a wine is corked?

You'll learn about this in Chapter 13. If in doubt when you are in a restaurant, ask the waiter to taste the wine for you.

What if I don't like the wine I've just bought in a restaurant?

If the wine is faulty, the restaurant should replace the bottle. If you find you often buy wines you don't like, spend more time talking to the waiter to establish what you are likely to enjoy. Explain what you like and see if you can find something similar. See Chapter 13 for more on this.

How do I get started?

Turn to Chapter 02 and start learning how to taste!

02

how to taste wine

In this chapter you will learn:
- how to set up a wine tasting and where to start
- the three easy steps of wine tasting
- how to write tasting notes
- the four key elements of wine
- how to taste horizontally, vertically and blind.

Becoming a wine taster: who can do it?

Many people think the ability to taste wine is something you are born with: you are either gifted as a taster or you are not. This is not true. Do you think you can taste the flavour of an apple as well as the next person? Can you tell if milk has turned sour? If someone put sugar in your coffee, would you notice? If the answer to these questions is 'yes', you can certainly taste wine. Another common view of novice tasters is that 'all wine tastes the same to me'. If you are one of those people, please read on. Once you learn to taste wine you will be amazed at just how different all those bottles lining the shelves of your local supermarket will taste. You *will* taste the difference.

Learning to taste is the single best skill you can acquire to enjoy wine more. The purpose of tasting (rather than drinking) wine is to try to understand why a wine tastes the way it does, and why you prefer one wine to another. When you taste you focus on the physical characteristics of the wine as well as the flavours you can taste. You will soon be able to tell good wine from bad, to judge whether a wine is ready to drink or might be better if kept for a while, and to understand the way a wine has been made. And most importantly, by focusing more closely on the tasting experience you will soon be able to define and refine your own individual taste, and choose the wines you like best.

Tasting wine is about harnessing the innate knowledge you already have, and then locking it in your memory for future use. Gifted wine tasters are invariably blessed with a good memory as much as a good palate, but developing both is within everyone's reach. As you do this, your newly heightened senses will reward you with greater appreciation of the food you eat as well as the wine you drink.

The magical sense of smell

The most important tool you have for tasting wine is your nose and the most important first step to becoming a proficient wine taster is to get yourself into the habit of smelling *everything* you taste.

Remember holding your nose to swallow medicine as a child? The medicine was bearable because, with a blocked sense of smell, the taste was also blocked. The taste buds on our tongues are blunt instruments compared to the thousands of smells we can recognize. It is our noses that guide us, and our palates that confirm what we smell.

Try this
Try this smell/taste test: hold a ripe pear under your nose and eat a piece of apple. The chances are you will taste pear in your mouth, not apple.

Starting out: choosing the right glass

Since the most important element of tasting is to be able to smell the wine, it is crucial to use a glass that enables you to do this effectively. Aromas are, by their very nature, volatile, and will escape from the glass. Therefore, you need to use a glass for wine tasting that keeps these aromas within your reach. It is also necessary to be able to swirl the liquid around to release more of the perfumes of the wine. The best kind of glass to use is one that has a sufficiently large bowl at the bottom to do this, and that curves inwards at the top, to capture the wine's scent. Once you start tasting and see what a difference it makes to use a glass that allows you better to taste the wine, you may well be abandoning all your other glasses in favour of this style of glassware.

Use a clear, uncut glass, so that you can see the wine. The fineness of the glass is of less importance, although thinner glass provides less of a barrier between you and the wine, so is usually preferred. Ultimately, the purpose of a tasting glass is to allow you the best, most neutral conditions to study a wine.

You will need several glasses, to enable you to compare one wine against another. The International Standards Organization has devised a glass specifically for wine tasting (commonly referred to as the ISO glass – see figure 1.1). These are sold in

figure 1.1 standard ISO tasting glass

boxes of six and are a useful and inexpensive investment. These days, many people prefer to use larger glasses than this for tasting, but as long as the glass conforms to the basic guidelines on shape, it will be fine.

It is a good idea, especially at first, when you are starting to taste, to use the same glasses every time. This will give you a useful point of reference, as your wine can taste quite different in different glasses.

Try this

Pour a small sample of the same wine into three different glasses, for example, a straight-sided water glass, a V-shaped wine glass (or cocktail glass) and a brandy bowl (or similar, bowl-shaped glass, or ISO tasting glass). Taking each glass in turn, swirl it, smell it and taste the wine. Do you notice any difference? Which do you prefer?

Tasting wine: three easy steps

1 Pour and observe.
2 Swirl and smell.
3 Taste and spit.

Try this

Buy a bottle of a wine you know and like, and have a sip of the wine just as you normally do. Now try tasting it following the steps below. See if you notice any difference in the wine when you taste it like this.

Pour and observe

Wine is best tasted at a cool room temperature. Chilling a wine will mute the aromas and flavours. It might taste better, but it will be more difficult to analyze. It is also easier to compare different wines if they are all the same temperature.

Pour a small amount of wine into the glass. This should be enough so that you can see the colour of the wine and take a good sip, but not so much that you have difficulty in swirling the wine freely. Around two good mouthfuls of wine is sufficient for a tasting measure. As a guide, you should be able to get 18–20 tasting measures from a 75 cl bottle. If you are using a larger glass, you will inevitably find you pour more than this.

Once you have poured the wine, tilt the glass slightly and look at the colour against a white background. Observe any gradations of colour. If the wine is young (say, one or two years old), it will probably look the same throughout. If it is older, it will probably look deepest in colour in the bottom of the glass and paler towards the edge you are tilting. This edge is known as the rim. It gives you an indication of how rapidly the wine is ageing. Red wines will become paler with age; white wines will darken. Some grape varieties are naturally paler than others and some wines age faster than others.

Swirl and smell

Next, smell the wine. There are a couple of ways to do this. Some people favour smelling the wine without first swirling the wine, to gain an initial impression of the wine. Do this if you like – you will see there is quite a difference when you then start to move the wine in the glass. I usually dispense with this step, however, and swirl the glass right away. Agitating wine without swirling it all over yourself can take a little practice. The easiest way to keep the wine in the glass is to keep the base of the glass on the table as you do this.

Don't be shy about sticking your nose right into the glass. This may not look very elegant, but it's the best way of smelling wine and is the way to taste like an expert from the start. Some wines will have aromas that positively leap from the glass. Others may require coaxing, by repeated swirling, or by warming the bowl of the glass in your hands (aromas become more volatile at higher temperatures). Of course, some wines just don't smell of much and there's nothing you can do about that.

Do spend time on this part of tasting. It may be hard to believe at first, but soon you will be able to learn almost everything you need to know about a wine before you even put it in your mouth.

Taste and spit

Finally, taste the wine. Take a good sip and hold the wine in your mouth for a second or two, noticing how it feels and tastes. Try to resist the urge to swallow it right away. Now start to move the wine gently around inside your mouth (this will certainly seem an unnatural thing to do). Notice what you taste and any sensations in different areas of your mouth. Does the wine taste as you expected from smelling it? If not, how does it differ?

After a few seconds, spit the wine out or swallow it. Notice the difference in your mouth once the wine has gone. What impression (if any) does it leave? Can you still taste it? This lingering sensation of flavour in the mouth is known as the finish, or length of a wine. A long finish is a sign of quality in a wine. Observe also the sensations in your mouth when you taste, and once you have spat out the wine. Do parts of your mouth feel dry? Can you feel your mouth watering?

Now repeat the tasting exercise. This time, once the wine is in your mouth, try drawing air into your mouth over the wine. This will take practice, and it will sound pretty disgusting, but it will probably enhance your ability to taste. The reason for doing this is that giving the wine air in your mouth opens up the wine's flavours even more and allows you to taste more elements of the wine. Don't worry if you can't master this at first (you may prefer to ignore this altogether); it won't spoil your enjoyment of tasting.

Tasting the four elements of wine

> ### Taste, don't drink
>
> Most people tend to swallow what they taste at first. This is not a problem if you are only going to taste one or two wines. But if you want to learn about wine tasting, you will want to taste several wines at one sitting. It's not compulsory to spit, but be aware that your critical faculties will diminish faster than you might expect if you swallow rather than spit. Spitting looks, sounds, and, frankly, *is* horrible, but it's essential if you want to learn about the differences between a range of wines. If you always swallow, you'll find the wines quickly all taste very similar. If you spit into an opaque jug or paper cup, it is a lot less unpleasant.

The four elements of wine are:

- fruit
- tannin
- acidity
- alcohol.

Together, these determine the balance of the wine. Tannins, acidity and alcohol make up the structure of the wine.

'Structure' is an understandably confusing term to use to describe a liquid. Think of structure as the non-flavour elements of a wine. The composition of a wine's fruit, alcohol, acid and tannin will determine its balance and quality. If you learn to identify these, you are well on your way to becoming a proficient wine taster.

Fruit

The fruit flavours come from the type of grapes that are used to make the wine (see Chapter 03). This provides the essential character of the wine. The grapes determine a wine's colour, the kind of aromas it has, whether it will taste sweet or dry, whether it will have flavours of peaches or blackcurrants or gooseberries. The fruit is the starting point for making wine.

> **Try these**
>
> Compare these two fruity, white wines:
>
> • highly fruity: Sauvignon Blanc from New Zealand
> • less fruity: Chablis from France (made from Chardonnay grapes).

Tannins

Tannins come from the skins and seeds of the grapes, and from the use of wood during winemaking. If you chew the skin of a grape, or a plum, you will have some idea of the contribution tannins make to wine. Wine grapes tend to have far thicker skins than table grapes and so higher levels of tannin. In the same way that tannins are invisible in tea, yet coat the sides of your mouth and cup, so the tannins in wine will deposit themselves on the inside of your mouth, creating a similar, drying effect. Swirling the wine around your mouth allows you better to taste the tannins in wine. After tasting relatively few red wines, you may notice your mouth and teeth becoming discoloured from tannins.

As white wines are fermented without grape skins, they contain little or no tannin, although if they have spent time in contact with wood during the winemaking process, they may have noticeable wood tannins, which can have a similar, mouth-puckering effect.

If a wine has a high level of tannins, it is described as tannic.

Try these

Compare the tannins in these two red wines:

- tannic: Chianti Classico from Tuscany, Italy
- less tannic: inexpensive Malbec from Argentina.

Acidity

Beginners often confuse acidity with tannins when learning to taste. The difference is that acidity freshens the mouth, making it water, whereas tannins have the reverse, drying effect. Both, however, provide structure to a wine. This means they support and complement the fruit to create a harmonious whole. White wines tend to be higher in acidity than red wines, partly because of the type of grapes from which white wines are made and partly because white wines rely on acidity for both their structure and freshness.

Acidity and sweetness

This is an important relationship to understand, as it affects the balance of many wines, in particular sweet wines. Here is an easy way to look at how acidity and sweetness work together – the *citron pressé* test.

Squeeze a lemon into a glass and add a little water. Taste it – if you can bear to. Now take a teaspoon of sugar and mix it in well. Taste the juice again. Keep adding sugar and tasting the drink. You might be surprised at how much sugar you need to add for the juice to be palatable. At some point, the sugar and the sharpness of the lemon should start to taste in balance. This shows how some very sweet wines can still taste balanced because they have sufficient acidity to keep them fresh. Now try adding the same amount of sugar to the same volume of liquid – this time, just water. When you taste this, you'll get some idea of how a sweet wine tastes when it has insufficient acidity to balance the sweetness.

Try these

Compare the acidity in these two white wines:

- acidic: Vinho Verde from Portugal
- less acidic: Gewurztraminer from Alsace, France.

Or, to see acidity in red wines use the comparison for tannic wines, above. The Chianti Classico will have much higher acidity than the Argentinian Malbec.

Alcohol

Wines that have high levels of alcohol will taste warm in the mouth (this is especially noticeable at the back of the mouth). The alcohol may also make the wine taste sweeter. Although alcohol doesn't have a specific aroma, you can often feel a spirity effect when smelling a high-alcohol wine. Most wines fall within the 12 per cent to 14.5 per cent band for alcohol by volume.

Try these

Compare the alcohol in these two red wines:

- higher alcohol: Shiraz from the Barossa Valley, Australia
- lower alcohol: red wine from the Loire Valley, France.

Learning to identify balance

The above examples indicate wines that tend to show high or low levels of the various components of wine. But this is not to say these wines are unbalanced. A wine made from Cabernet Sauvignon grapes will always have more natural tannins than a wine made from Pinot Noir grapes, for example, but both can be in balance and equally good in terms of quality.

Once you have learnt to distinguish between tannins, acidity and alcohol in wine, it is easier to determine if these elements are present to excess, or in insufficient amounts, in a wine. For example, a red wine with very low alcohol may lack weight in the mouth and feel unsatisfying, whereas a very high level of alcohol will tend to dull the flavours and aromas of the fruit and leave a burning sensation in the mouth. If a wine has low levels of tannin it may seem insubstantial – more like fruit juice than wine. Excessive tannins, though, will leave the mouth very dry. A wine with low acidity may seem flat and tiring to drink.

Acidity gives wine its refreshment quality, but a wine that is too acidic will be hard to drink: a little like the difference between drinking melon juice and lemon juice.

The key to understanding balance is to be able to identify how the different elements in wine interact with each other to create the whole. Perception of balance will depend on personal tolerance and preferences, as well as an understanding of how different wines naturally taste. Alcohol, acidity and tannins are important in determining a wine's ability to age, and when it should be drunk.

Knowing if a wine is ready to drink

Once wine is sealed in a bottle, it continues to change over time. Most wines are ready to drink just as soon as they are bottled, so that you can enjoy their fresh fruitiness. If a wine tastes good, it's almost certainly a good time to drink it. But some wines are only at their best after a period of bottle ageing.

The usual beneficial effect of time on the taste of a wine is to soften it, and make it easier to drink. Tannins, oak and acid become less obvious, due to the many chemical changes that take place in the bottle. The character of the fruit changes, too. Young wine tastes and smells of fresh fruit, but it evolves over time to present a less fruity but broader spectrum of flavours. Some wines are best left for a few months to a year in bottle, and a few can improve for a decade or more in bottle, if stored correctly.

Each wine will have its own optimal 'drinking window', after which time its quality will decline. For more on this, read about storing wine, in Chapter 14. For the purposes of tasting notes, think about how the different elements of the wine seem to you now and make a guess at how they might evolve. This is very difficult. Even the most experienced tasters are guessing when they give estimated drinking dates for wines. And to confuse things further, personal taste is a crucial element of this. Some people prefer younger wine, while others like it older. The only way to work out what it is that *you* like is to keep trying the same wines over time to see how they age. Some grape varieties, and some wine regions, produce wines that will age for longer than others, as you will see in subsequent Chapters 03 to 07.

Tasting practice

For most of us, it is more economical and practical to taste in a group. It's also useful because everyone will have a different tasting experience, and it is instructive to hear a variety of opinions on the same wine.

Start by learning about the taste of some of the most common grape varieties, and move on to different wine styles, to see how climate and winemaking affect the flavours in wine. (This is explained further in Chapters 04 and 05; to understand more about the different varieties before you get started, turn first to Chapter 03.) Some examples of classic grape varieties to get started with are listed below.

Try to use as many glasses as you have wines, so that you can compare what you taste. Compare wines side by side to increase the speed of your learning. It's much easier to see differences between two or more wines than to look at one wine in isolation. Start with two, three or four wines. As you become more experienced at tasting, you can increase this number, but with fewer wines it is easier to focus on all the elements of each one. It's a good idea to leave some wine in each glass after you have tasted it to allow you to go back and taste it later. Often, wines change with exposure to the air.

Classic grape varieties

The following chapter gives more detail on how grape varieties taste, but first, try these tastings to see the differences for yourself.

Try these

Try these three white wines from grape varieties that should taste quite different:

- Sauvignon Blanc – New Zealand
What you'll find ... a blast of fruit, gooseberries, grass, nettles, blackcurrant leaves, powerful aromas and mouthwatering, fresh flavours.

- Chardonnay – USA
What you'll find ... melony, peachy, ripe fruit aromas and flavours. Probably less strongly aromatic than the Sauvignon Blanc.

Maybe seems less fresh than the Sauvignon (due to lower acidity), might taste creamy, buttery, rich, or oaky/woody (if an oaked style of wine). Might feel heavier in your mouth.

• Riesling – Germany

What you'll find … strong aromas, but probably less powerful than the New Zealand wine. May be slightly sweet, although you may not notice this, due to the high acidity of the wine. Lighter in weight and alcohol compared to the other two wines.

Try these

Try these classic red wine varieties:

• Cabernet Sauvignon – Maipo Valley, Chile

What you'll find … pure, ripe, blackcurrant fruit, maybe with some minty notes as well. More expensive wines will probably have some oaky aromas. You'll notice the firm Cabernet tannins here.

• Pinot Noir – California, USA

What you'll find … rich, ripe, strawberry- and raspberry-flavoured fruit. Softly-structured, with no harsh tannins. Easy to enjoy.

• Shiraz – McLaren Vale, Australia

What you'll find … powerful, black fruit and sweet chocolate flavours, probably with toasty oak, coconut and grilled meat aromas. High in alcohol and full in the mouth.

When comparing wines, remember to look for differences in colour, aromatic intensity and flavour. Ask yourself questions. What aromas are present? Do the wines smell fruity, floral, woody, grassy, mineral? Which is the most acidic? Do the wines differ in their weight in the mouth? Which has the highest alcohol? Can you taste this?

Notes and scores

No matter how good a memory you have, you will need to make a note of the wines you taste. You can create your own tasting sheets, or just record your thoughts in a notebook. An example of the information you might include on a tasting sheet, or in a notebook, is shown below, indicating the name of the wine, its appearance, the impression you get when you smell and taste it, and any conclusions you want to add. By taking this sort of systematic approach to tasting from the outset, you will soon have a record of how wines differ according to grape variety, wine region and producer. You'll also be building up a bank of wines that you know and you will start to identify which wines you tend to prefer.

A good tasting note can be subjective, objective or both. A combination of the two is perhaps the most useful, as it shows the objectively identifiable characteristics of the wine and what you think of it.

Giving scores to wine is strangely contentious. Some people (including many wine producers) dislike scores because they feel a wine should not be reduced to a single number. My view is that if a score helps you to distinguish between one wine and the next, it is a good thing – and it does not prevent you from writing a flowery description as well if you want to. Some people score out of 10, 20, or 100. Others have highly complicated scoring systems, giving separate marks according to the wine's appearance, smell and taste. When I am tasting a lot of wines where there are bound to be many that are similar, I use a score, a tasting note and a further symbol to remind myself if I really liked the wine, in a purely subjective way (I tend to think of this as the 'deliciousness' quotient of the wine). Do whatever works for you. You'll probably find that this is a process that becomes easier the more wines you taste, as you learn to identify their distinguishing factors and which wines you enjoy.

Sample tasting sheet

Date

Wine
Name of producer, region, country, vintage, price

Appearance
Colour – what colour? Is it light/dark/pale/intense/transparent/opaque? Does it have bubbles? Is there any sediment?

Nose
What do you smell? Is it attractive or unattractive? Is it intense, pungent, mild, fresh, stale? Describe the aromas. Are they herbal, floral, vegetal, animal, fruity, oaky? Be as precise as you can.

Palate
How does the wine feel in your mouth? Does it taste as you expected? Describe the flavours – are they intense? Are they the same as the nose? What about tannins? Are they hard or soft?

Do you notice acidity? Or alcohol? Can you detect oak? Do you notice one aspect of the wine more than others? How about the texture and weight of fruit? Does the wine seem ready to drink now? Do you like it? When you have swallowed or spat out the wine, does the flavour remain in your mouth?

Conclusion
What is your overall impression of the wine? Do you think it is in balance? Do you like it? Is it ready to drink? If not, how long do you think you should wait? Or is it too old? What about the price? Do you think it is worth the money? Is it representative of its style? Would you buy it again?

Help! I have nothing to say ...

A tasting note can be as long or as short as you like. Don't worry about not having the 'right' vocabulary to describe wine. You will soon find words, or signs, that work for you. And hopefully, the more you taste, the more you will distinguish between the flavours and aromas of different styles of wine described in this book. Here's an example of a tasting note for a wine from Argentina, made from Malbec grapes and costing £6.

Wine
Name of producer, name of wine, vintage, per cent alcohol, price

Appearance
Deep, opaque, purple colour.

Nose
Fruity nose, with violets and some coconut aromas over dark berry fruits; aromatic and appealing.

Palate
Full weight of ripe, juicy fruit, soft tannins and refreshing acidity. The fruit character is intense, and although it lacks great complexity, the wine has good balance between fruit, acidity, alcohol and tannins and the flavours are deliciously ripe.

Conclusion
This is a good quality wine that is ready to drink. It shows the youthful, juicy, black fruit character one would expect from Argentina and it offers good value for money.

A few tasting ideas

You'll find many more examples for comparative and illustrative tastings in the chapters that follow, but here are some ideas to start with.

- **One grape variety from a number of countries.** For example, Cabernet Sauvignon from California, France, Australia, Chile. See Chapter 03 for examples of what grows where and what to compare, and Chapter 04 for the influence of a country's climate on the taste of wine.
- **Different varieties from one country.** For example, try Riesling, Sauvignon Blanc, Pinot Gris, Pinot Noir and a Cabernet/Merlot blend from New Zealand. See Chapters 08 and 09 for more tasting ideas by country.
- **Oaked versus unoaked wines.** Try oaked and unoaked Chardonnay, Sauvignon Blanc and American Fumé Blanc (which means oaked Sauvignon Blanc), and a young versus an aged Rioja to learn about the influence of oak. See Chapter 05 for more examples of wines to taste to see the influence of the winemaker, and the wide range of flavours associated with oak.

Horizontal and vertical tastings

These can be fun to do. A horizontal tasting is a tasting of a number of wines all from the same vintage. A vertical tasting is the same wine tasted over a number of vintages.

Tasting 'blind'

Blind tasting refers to the practice of covering the bottle so that you don't know the identity of the wine when you taste it. It can be fun to try to guess what a wine might be, but the main value of blind tasting is as a learning tool. Removed from the influence of the label, you are reliant purely on your own senses to judge the wine in your glass. It is a powerful way to concentrate the mind. Try to taste blind whenever you can. Even if you know what the wines are that you have bought, try to mix them up and cover them with foil or a bag. You will get a lot more out of tasting this way.

part

two

the flavours of wine

03

grape varieties

In this chapter you will learn:
- how grapes affect the flavour of wine
- how to identify the grapes in a wine from the label (even when they are not listed)
- the defining characteristics of the major grape varieties.

The most important influence on the flavour of a wine is the grape variety, or varieties, from which it is made. Knowing the grape variety of a wine should give you a good indication of the wine's character, so it is a good starting point to get to know the major varieties you will find.

Almost all of the quality wine produced in the world is made from grapes of the European vine species, *Vitis vinifera*. There are thousands of varieties of *vinifera*, but relatively few are commonly seen on wine labels. Best known are the 'international' varieties that are planted throughout the world. For the most part, they are French in origin. These include Cabernet Sauvignon, Chardonnay, Sauvignon Blanc, Merlot, Pinot Noir and Syrah. Some countries, notably Italy and Portugal, have many indigenous varieties that are rarely seen elsewhere. This chapter focuses on the main varieties you are likely to come across. At the end of the chapter, you will find a reference showing the likely composition of grape varieties in commonly found wines that rarely give any clues about what grapes they are made from on the label.

Why grapes?

What makes grapes the best fruit for wine? The key features necessary for successful transformation of grapes into wine are sugar, acids and phenolic compounds. These are found in the flesh, the skin and the seeds of the grapes. Wine grapes tend to be smaller than table grapes. They have thicker skins, a greater number of pips and higher levels of natural acidity. These physical properties make them better suited to fermentation, as they have greater concentration of flavour.

Sugar

Sugar is essential for alcoholic fermentation to take place. Compared with other fruits, grapes have high sugar levels (around 25 per cent of grape juice is sugar), which is an essential requirement for successful fermentation. Grapes contain two sugars, glucose and fructose. Approximately 17 grams of sugar are required to produce one degree of alcohol.

Acids

Grapes are unusual in that they contain high levels of natural acids as well as sugar. Acidity is important in giving wine freshness: it is the acidity in wine that makes your mouth water when you drink it and invites you to take another sip. The main acids in grapes are tartaric acid and malic acid. As grapes ripen, their level of acidity falls. As certain varieties of grapes have higher natural acid levels than others, these are often chosen for making wine in hot climates, where acid levels in ripe grapes tend to be low.

Phenolic compounds

These are found principally in the skins of the grapes. Phenolic compounds give wine colour, aroma, flavour and tannin. Tannins are easily tasted in grapes. Try chewing on a grape skin to experience the mouth-puckering and tooth-coating effects of tannins in your mouth, similar to that of an over-brewed cup of black tea. You may also notice that, beneath the dry tannins, these skins contain more flavour than the pulp.

The drying sensation of tannins is not pleasant in isolation, but the right amount of tannin, when combined with the other elements in the grapes, will give red wines balance, structure and intensity of flavour. Tannins also contain natural antioxidants, so they help to preserve wine in bottle. This is why red wines tend to age better than whites. Red wines contain varying amounts of grape tannins, depending on the type of grapes from which they are made, the conditions where the grapes were grown and how long the wine spends in contact with the grape skins during the winemaking process.

How do you know what kind of grapes a wine is made from?

Many wines will state the variety, or varieties, from which they are made on the label. If only one variety is stated, the wine will be made either 100 per cent from that variety, or it may be mostly from that variety (usually at least 85 per cent but this depends on local labelling laws), plus a smaller proportion of other grape varieties. If two varieties are stated on the label, for example, Cabernet Sauvignon/Merlot, the first grape mentioned will be the more important grape in the blend.

In many parts of the world there is no mention of the grape variety on the label. The wine is simply labelled by its region and country of origin. This tends to be the norm in traditional wine-producing parts of the world, such as France, Italy and Spain. With their long histories of wine production, certain regions, towns and villages have become renowned for the quality of their wines. For example, more people are familiar with the name 'Rioja' than Tempranillo, the main grape variety used in its production. And Saint-Emilion is undoubtedly a more valuable tool for selling a wine than simply stating that the wine is a blend of Merlot and Cabernet Sauvignon, a grape combination that can be found in countless other places.

It is often the case that the wine law in traditional regions prohibits any mention of the grape variety on the front label, on the grounds that it is the particular characteristics of the region that give the wine its distinctive qualities, rather than the grape variety. To some extent it is true that the uniqueness of each place where grapes are grown will give nuances of difference to the wines of that place – there is no other Chardonnay like Chablis, for example – but in most cases, the distinctive qualities of the grape varieties are perceptible, whether or not they are written on the bottle.

Why do wines from the same grape variety taste different?

The descriptions below are intended to give you pointers to how wines made from different varieties typically taste, but there are inevitably differences between wines made from the same grape variety. This may be explained by a number of things. One is the size of the crop (or yield), which can greatly influence how much a wine tastes of the grapes from which it is made. A restricted yield will tend to produce grapes, and therefore wines, with more concentrated flavours. Similarly, an older vine will often give grapes that have more complex flavours than a younger vine. This is why some wines have 'old vines' (or *vieilles vignes*) mentioned on the label. What constitutes an old vine, or a low yield, is up to the individual producer to decide (but is typically at least 25 years old). Some vine varieties are far more sensitive to yields and vine age than others. Other factors to consider are the climate in which the grapes were grown (see Chapter 04) and the influence of the winemaker (see Chapter 05).

Most important grape varieties

Below are the most important varieties you will find in wines across the world.

Red wine grapes

Cabernet Sauvignon

Probably the world's best-known grape variety, Cabernet Sauvignon manages to retain its distinctive personality wherever it is grown. The grapes are small and thick-skinned, with a large number of pips. They produce wines that have high colour and tannins and are often well suited to ageing. Because of Cabernet's firm structure, it is often blended with softer, fleshier varieties, notably Merlot. The most long-lived red wines of Bordeaux are produced predominantly from this winning combination.

Key distinguishing features: blackcurrant, herbal, eucalyptus aromas and flavours; plenty of tannin and colour; firm structure.

Where to find it: widespread, but especially France (Bordeaux, Languedoc), Spain, Chile, Australia, South Africa, USA (California), Bulgaria.

Pinot Noir

The grape of Burgundy, from which all the region's best red wines are exclusively made, Pinot Noir is admired for its heady perfume and stylish elegance. Never heavy, Pinot Noir can delight in its youth, yet age as well as any other variety, despite its apparent frailty. In contrast to Cabernet Sauvignon's deep colour and firm tannins, Pinot Noir is usually rather pale in colour – ruby rather than purple – with gentle levels of tannin. Unfortunately, it is a difficult grape to grow, and although winemakers throughout the world struggle to craft memorable wines from Pinot Noir, there are rather more undistinguished than distinguished bottles available. Hence, good Pinot Noir usually comes with a luxury price tag. Burgundy still reigns supreme for the range of quality wines from Pinot Noir, but it is increasingly being challenged by New Zealand. Pinot Noir is rarely blended with other varieties, and certainly never for serious wines: why would anyone want to dilute the character of something so special?

Key distinguishing features: red fruit and floral aromas, silky texture, refreshing acidity, maddeningly irregular in quality.

Where to find it: not widespread; hard to grow; France (Burgundy), New Zealand, Chile, USA (Oregon, California), Germany.

Syrah/Shiraz

These two names are used interchangeably, but both are the same grape. This variety gives highly coloured wines with plenty of tannins, but compared to Cabernet Sauvignon, the tannins tend to be softer and the wines approachable earlier. In warmer climates it is often blended with Cabernet Sauvignon, where it does a similar job to Merlot, softening Cabernet's tendency to austerity. While the flavours of the two grapes are similar, the firmness of Cabernet's structure complements the rounder, fleshier Syrah. The best wines are usually not blended with other grapes. Occasionally, you may find Syrah blended with a small quantity of (white) Viognier grapes. Syrah is the only black grape used in wines from the northern Rhône. Wine producers often label their wine Syrah or Shiraz depending on the style of wine they are making. More restrained, peppery, European-style wines tend to be labelled Syrah; more upfront, fruit-driven, bold, Australian styles are more likely to be called Shiraz.

Key distinguishing features: deep purple colour; blackcurrant, black pepper, black cherry, chocolate, spice and leather aromas and flavours; juicy fruit; generous weight of fruit and alcohol; good weight of tannins, but rounder and sweeter than Cabernet.

Where to find it: widespread, especially in the new world: France (Rhône, southern France), Australia, USA (California, Washington), Chile, Argentina, South Africa, New Zealand.

Merlot

Often blended with Cabernet to add succulence and weight of fruit, Merlot is the main ingredient in most of the wines from Saint-Emilion (and other Right Bank appellations) in Bordeaux. These are wines known for their smoothness and easy appeal. Less distinguished examples of Merlot can be light and fruity, or soft and bland.

Key distinguishing features: deep colour; plum and blackcurrant flavours; usually supple tannins; approachable early.

Where to find it: very common, often blended. France (Bordeaux and south west), Italy, USA, New Zealand, Chile.

Grenache/Garnacha

This is the same variety, depending on whether you are in France or Spain. Widely planted in Spain, it produces wines that tend to be pale in colour, with high levels of alcohol and sweet, jammy fruit. Often combined with Syrah in the southern Rhône in France, Grenache is the main grape in Châteauneuf-du-Pape and most of the wines labelled Côtes du Rhône.

Key distinguishing features: sweetly fruity; tends to be high in alcohol; fruit-forward; soft tannins and acidity; usually pale in colour.

Where to find it: France (southern Rhône, southern France), Spain, Australia.

White wine grapes

Chardonnay

Best known from Burgundy, though its name rarely features on any label in Burgundy, Chardonnay is often referred to as the winemaker's grape. This is because it is easily fashioned into different styles of wine. It happily grows in a range of climates – almost everywhere grapes are planted – but it produces its most elegant expression in cooler sites, where it retains its crispness and, sometimes, mineral flavours. Chardonnay has been something of a victim of fashion, produced in big, oaky styles, or – more recently – in slimline, oak-free versions, according to the whims of the market and those who make it. In Burgundy it is always produced as a single varietal wine. Elsewhere it is blended with various grape varieties, such as Sémillon. It is the only white grape variety in Champagne, where it forms part of the blend with Pinot Noir and Pinot Meunier, or is produced as a single varietal, labelled 'Blanc de blancs' (white wine from white grapes).

Key distinguishing features: often heavily influenced by winemaking, notably to impart oaky and creamy characters and texture; flavours include melon, peach, lemon, apples, flint and minerals.

Where to find it: everywhere.

Sauvignon Blanc

One of the easiest grapes to get to know, Sauvignon's unmistakably powerful aroma gives away its identity every time. Traditionally from the Loire Valley in France, it is the sole grape of Sancerre, Pouilly Fumé and several less well-known appellations, where its identity is hidden behind the name of the commune where it is grown. More recently it has found fame in New Zealand, where it accounts for the majority of the country's production. Sauvignon has uncomplicated appeal and strong, upfront flavours that recall gooseberries, grass and elderflowers. Best known as a single varietal wine, it is also commonly blended with Sémillon, whose lemony, waxy flavours add texture and interest to the sometimes one-dimensional Sauvignon. It is also sometimes vinified using oak, which lends a smoky character to its wines.

Key distinguishing features: pungent aromas; flavours range from green to tropical; crisp acidity; bright and fruity.

Where to find it: widespread, especially France (Loire Valley and Bordeaux), New Zealand, South Africa, Chile.

Riesling

Another highly aromatic variety, Riesling wines are mainly distinguished by their always-fresh acidity. They are also often low in alcohol, and this combination makes Riesling the source of some of the most refreshing wines to be found. Riesling reaches its greatest heights in Germany, where it is produced all across the country. It is a versatile grape that can be made into many styles of wine, from bone dry to richly sweet. Unlike Sauvignon, Rieslings are often made to age. With maturity, their aromas change from fresh, floral and mineral to savoury, diesel and sometimes toasty aromas (although the latter is rarely derived from oak toastiness). Riesling performs best in cooler climates, but is widely grown. It is usually vinified alone.

Key distinguishing features: high acidity; perfumed, floral aromas; light-bodied; often sweet; good quality.

Where to find it: Germany, France (Alsace), Australia, Austria, New Zealand, USA (New York and Washington states).

Other important grape varieties

The varieties below are less important internationally, but are often highly significant for a region, being the major, or sole, source of grapes for the wines produced. They are organized according to the country where you are most likely to find them.

Red wine grapes

France

Cabernet Franc

Not often seen on a label as an individual variety, this grape is often found as a minor player in 'Bordeaux blends' alongside Cabernet Sauvignon and Merlot. Cabernet Franc ripens more easily than Cabernet Sauvignon and could be considered a lighter version of the grape. Most appealing is its fragrance, which can range from violets to pencil shavings. It is best known as a solo performer in the red wines of the Loire (Chinon, Saumur, Saumur-Champigny, Bourgeuil), where its quality is heavily dependent on the vintage (see Chapter 04 for more on the influence of climate on wine).

Key distinguishing features: highly aromatic (floral, woody, elegant); character similar to Cabernet Sauvignon, but lighter and fruitier; can be herbaceous; has chalky tannins when grown in France's Loire Valley.

Where to find it: France (Loire Valley, Bordeaux); limited examples in the new world, but can be very good.

Gamay

The grape of Beaujolais, *nouveau* or otherwise, Gamay's character varies according to the quality of the wine. It is, however, always bright and fruit-driven. Wines range from light, early drinking styles, with bubblegum flavours, to more age-worthy, serious styles that have greater concentration and that have been matured in oak to add complexity of flavour. Some light Gamay, red and rosé, is found in the Loire Valley, but little elsewhere.

Key distinguishing features: purple colour, succulent red fruit character, fresh acidity and moderate alcohol.

Where to find it: France (Beaujolais, Loire Valley).

Mourvèdre

A late-ripening variety that needs a warm autumn to give of its best, Mourvèdre is a quality grape that produces wines of dense concentration and gamey richness. It is an important grape in southern France and Spain.

Key distinguishing features: deep colour; animal, spicy aromas; black fruit character; makes interesting wines.

Where to find it: southern France, especially Bandol, Spain (where it is known as Monastrell).

Italy

Nebbiolo

The sole grape of Barolo and Barbaresco, many consider Nebbiolo to be the raw material of the finest wines of Italy. Native to Piedmont, in north west Italy, where it still produces the best wines, it is a difficult grape to grow, which probably explains producers' reluctance to plant it elsewhere. Nebbiolo produces highly distinctive wines and needs no other variety to add to its character. Nebbiolo wines are powerful and long-lived. Usually pale in colour, Nebbiolo is known for its hauntingly lovely aromas, which can range from flowers (typically roses) to leather and tar. The wines are often hard to approach when young, due to their high levels of tannin.

Key distinguishing features: pale in colour; beautifully aromatic; challenging structure; wines need time in bottle to soften.

Where to find it: Italy (Piedmont).

Barbera

Another grape from Piedmont, Barbera is widely planted in Italy and known for its freshness and bright, red fruit flavours. Its acidity makes it a refreshing accompaniment to food.

Key distinguishing features: ruby colour; high acidity; sour cherry and plum flavours; fairly low tannins.

Where to find it: Italy (Piedmont), Argentina.

Dolcetto

An important grape in Piedmont, Dolcetto makes wines that are deep in colour and full-flavoured. Their simple fruitiness makes them best suited for early consumption.

Key distinguishing features: deep purple colour; relatively low acidity; crisp tannins.

Where to find it: Italy (Piedmont).

Sangiovese

The best-known grape of Tuscany, Sangiovese is the quality driver in Chianti, where it can constitute up to 100 per cent of the blend. It goes under many synonyms locally (Brunello and

Morellino, for example). Sangiovese wines are distinctive, combining intense fruitiness with fierce tannins and good levels of acidity and alcohol. Despite its widespread use in Italian wine, is not widely grown elsewhere.

Key distinguishing features: plum, cherry and leather aromas; high tannins and acidity; quite light colour.

Where to find it: Italy (Tuscany), Argentina.

Nero d'Avola

This Italian grape is from Sicily, where it is the most planted red grape. Quality varies, but the best wines are juicy and plummy, with good structure.

Key distinguishing features: deep in colour; richly fruity; firm structure; good acidity.

Where to find it: Sicily, southern Italy.

Negroamaro

This southern Italian grape produces deeply coloured (though not bitter, as the name suggests) wines for early consumption. Their generous fruit and alcohol reflect the warm growing conditions of the south.

Key distinguishing features: deep colour; ripe, often raisined fruit character; warm alcohol.

Where to find it: southern Italy.

Spain

Tempranillo

This quality grape is native to Spain and the major ingredient in the wines from Rioja (where it is usually blended with Grenache, among others) and Ribera del Duero (where it is known as Tinto Fino). It is also widely grown in Portugal. The wines have good fruit but can be low in acidity.

Key distinguishing features: ripe, strawberry fruit, often with vanilla flavours from oak; can be pale or dark in colour, depending on where it is grown.

Where to find it: Spain, Portugal (called Aragonez or Tinta Roriz), Argentina.

Portugal

Touriga Nacional

This top-quality grape is used to make port and many of the best red table wines of Portugal. Touriga Nacional's small berries produce deeply-coloured, concentrated, tannic wines that are perfectly suited to port production. It is usually blended when used to make table wines, where its elegance, perfume and class are easily seen.

Key distinguishing features: intense colour and concentrated flavours; tannic, long-lived, high class; Portugal's best grape.

Where to find it: Portugal.

Argentina

Malbec

Originally from Bordeaux, Malbec is now best-known from Argentina, where it produces brilliantly drinkable, deeply-coloured reds at all quality levels. It is often found as a single varietal, but is also suited to blending with less supple varieties, such as Cabernet Sauvignon. It is increasingly found in Chile, and it is the major grape in the wines of Cahors, in south west France, where it is known as Côt. It is less often seen in Bordeaux now, as the variety thrives best in drier climatic conditions, such as those found in Argentina.

Key distinguishing features: dark purple colour; sweet and floral (violets), lifted aromas often complemented by oak; ripe, black fruit flavours; gentle tannins.

Where to find it: Argentina, south west France (Cahors), Chile.

South Africa

Pinotage

South Africa's own grape, Pinotage is a firm divider of opinions as to its quality. This is a cross-bred grape, derived from Pinot Noir and Cinsault, though it displays little of the breed of its illustrious parent, Pinot Noir, and more of the workaday character of Cinsault. Pinotage is produced in a range of styles in South Africa, but the grape has failed to ignite interest elsewhere.

Key distinguishing features: individual, but divisive; richly fruity, often shows banana, plasticky, or paint aromas that some find offputting.

Where to find it: South Africa.

Chile

Carmenère

Another old and abandoned Bordeaux variety, Carmenère was brought to Chile by pioneer winemakers in the nineteenth century, and it is still widely grown today. Long mislabelled as Merlot, Carmenère is thankfully now a regular sight on Chilean wine labels. It is also responsible for some of the most exciting wines coming from Chile today, either as a single varietal wine, or blended with other Bordeaux varieties, such as Cabernet Sauvignon.

Key distinguishing features: scents of tobacco and spice, sometimes green or leafy if less ripe; fleshy fruit; can be high quality.

Where to find it: Chile.

Uruguay

Tannat

As the name suggests, Tannat is a highly tannic variety that can produce good quality wines. Its structure makes it a useful blending ingredient, although it is also seen as a single varietal wine.

Key distinguishing features: deep colour; high tannins; black fruit; can be rather one-dimensional.

Where to find it: south west France (Madiran), Uruguay.

USA

Zinfandel

Known as 'California's grape', where it has a fanatical following, 'Zin' is rarely found elsewhere (although it is genetically identical to Primitivo, found in southern Italy). Zinfandel wines are bold, fruity and alcoholic, sometimes reaching alcohol levels of 16 per cent or more. It is also found in a pink version (called, a little confusingly, 'white Zinfandel'), when it will be lower in alcohol, lightly fruity and with some residual sweetness.

Key distinguishing features: sweet fruit, often with chocolate, black cherry flavours and a noticeable raisined character; often spicy; usually high in alcohol and fairly low in colour.

Where to find it: USA (California).

White wine grapes

France

Sémillon

Most often seen as a single varietal wine when grown in Australia, Sémillon is also commonly partnered with Sauvignon Blanc or Chardonnay. Depending on the climate where it is grown, Sémillon can be dry, light and crisp, or full-bodied and round. Its flavours are in the spectrum of lemon, honey and beeswax. It is often used to make sweet wines, most notably in Sauternes, where it is the main grape in the blend. The honeyed character of the fruit and its susceptibility to noble rot make it well suited to sweet wines.

Key distinguishing features: zesty lemon flavours; usually only medium weight; richer styles often have a waxy character.

Where to find it: Australia, France (Bordeaux).

Viognier

Viognier's reputation was built on the high-quality wines it produces in Condrieu, the northern Rhône appellation whose wines are made exclusively from this variety. It is also grown in other parts of France, and the new world, but the wines rarely match the intensity of flavour and aroma of those produced from the fruit of the low-yielding vines of Condrieu. Viognier is rich but usually dry. The wines are full-bodied, with a heady, apricot scent. More commercial styles of Viognier sometimes capture the aromas of the best wines, but the magical essence of the grape is invariably lost. It's worth searching out good examples of this fine grape.

Key distinguishing features: weighty; high in alcohol; silky texture; perfumed and rich.

Where to find it: France (Condrieu and the south), USA, Australia, Chile.

Chenin Blanc

Widely produced in France's Loire Valley, but little found elsewhere, the exception being South Africa, where it is the most planted grape. Chenin Blanc is made in a wide variety of styles, from sparkling to dry, medium-dry, medium-sweet and lusciously sweet. It is often described as having the aroma of wet wool, which sometimes translates as musty, dank and not altogether pleasant. More attractive aromas include honey, lemon and apples. At high yields, the variety produces wines that are crisp and anonymous; grown on the chalky soils of the Loire Valley, its flavours gain in intensity and interest. As it is susceptible to noble rot, it is often made into sweet wines, some of which are of the highest quality.

Key distinguishing features: crisp acidity; highly variable quality; honeyed, appley fruit.

Where to find it: France, South Africa.

Muscat

This is a grape that comes in many guises – sweet, dry, fizzy and fortified – but all bear the trademark, grapey smell that identifies them as Muscat. Wines from Muscat tend to be pale in colour and low in acidity. Their aroma is often more pronounced than their flavour. Not the most fashionable of grapes, it is the source of some of the world's more distinctive styles, such as Moscato d'Asti from Italy, the rich, raisined, Rutherglen Muscats of Australia and the sweet, fortified Vins Doux Naturels from southern France.

Key distinguishing features: pale in colour; low in acid; fruity and often sweet.

Where to find it: France, Italy, Australia, Spain.

Gewurztraminer

Possibly the easiest grape to identify blind, nothing smells quite like Gewurztraminer. It has an exotic, heady perfume of lychees, roses and spice (the German word *Gewürz* translates as 'spice'). Some people adore it, but Gewurztraminer is simply too much for many people. Naturally deep in colour, it is full-bodied and tends to have high alcohol. Due to the variety's tendency to rapid accumulation of sugar, wines from Gewurztraminer often have some residual sugar. Even when there is no residual sugar, their intensity and richness often make the wines appear sweet. The most full-bodied examples of the grape are found in Alsace, where the wines are often produced in a late-harvest, sweet style. Due to its low acidity, these wines are usually best when young. Lighter, more floral versions of the grape are found elsewhere, such as in the Alto Adige region of northern Italy. New world Gewurztraminer also tends to be lighter. Some producers have experimented with adding acidity, or blending the grape with crisper varieties, such as Riesling, to create alternative styles.

Key distinguishing features: richly scented; deep in colour; low acidity; high alcohol; often sweet.

Where to find it: France, Italy, pockets of the new world.

Italy

Pinot Gris/Pinot Grigio

This is the same grape – but in two different styles. The Italian style and restaurant favourite, Pinot Grigio makes soft, easy wines of watery appearance, often with a touch of sweetness. These wines are unchallenging and, for the most part, uninteresting, but admirably good at not diverting your attention from your food or company. With lower yields, Pinot Gris can be made into something altogether more alluring. In Alsace and New Zealand, Pinot Gris can be a richly textured wine, with spicy, peachy aromas and oily intensity. Here, too, it can be sweet, often very sweet, but the most usual style is from dry to off-dry.

Key distinguishing features: smooth-textured; off-dry; peaches-and-cream fruit; can be rich or bland.

Where to find it: France, Italy, New Zealand, USA.

Spain

Albariño

A quality grape from northern Spain, good Albariño combines Viognier's aromas with Riesling's zesty acidity. The wines are generally of good to high quality and well balanced.

Key distinguishing features: apricot and peach aromas; medium-bodied, balanced; crisp.

Where to find it: Spain, Portugal (as Alvarinho).

Verdejo

From the Rueda region, Verdejo produces delightfully fresh, lemony and grassy wines.

Key distinguishing features: pale colour; zesty freshness.

Where to find it: Spain.

Austria

Grüner Veltliner

Invariably delicious wines are made from Grüner Veltliner, which is the most important grape in Austria. The wines have full, fruity concentration, but are not heavy or overdone. It is usually a reliable restaurant choice.

Key distinguishing features: full and dry; distinctive white pepper aromas and smooth fruit; high quality.

Where to find it: Austria.

Greece

Assyrtiko

High-quality, dry and mineral wines are made from Assyrtiko, coming mainly from the island of Santorini.

Key distinguishing features: crisp and mineral; good balance; original.

Where to find it: Greece.

Hungary

Furmint

Furmint is the major grape of Hungary's best wine, the lusciously sweet Tokaj. Furmint is also made into dry wines. While less exciting than the sweet wines, these dry and semi-dry wines are respectable and all have brisk levels of acidity.

Key distinguishing features: highly acidic; lots of character, especially when made into sweet Tokaj wine.

Where to find it: Hungary.

Other grape varieties

Carignan (red)

This widely planted and high-yielding grape variety can produce interesting wines from old vines, but basic examples are otherwise more common. It is often blended with more characterful varieties, which have in many cases come to replace it, especially in the south of France. It is known as Cariñena or Mazuela in Spain.

Petit Verdot (red)

This is a minor but important, late-ripening variety found in Bordeaux. The small percentage used by many producers adds colour, tannin and spice to a blend.

Macabeo (white)

This is a widely planted grape, also known as Viura, in Spain. It makes largely undistinguished but clean white wines.

Trebbiano (white)

Trebbiano is a variety common in Italy, where it produces anonymous, light, white wines. It is also widely planted in France, where it is known as Ugni Blanc.

Marsanne (white)

This is a good quality grape variety for Rhône whites, and is also found in Australia.

Roussanne (white)

Roussane is another quality and age-worthy grape of the Rhône. It has an attractive herbal character and good levels of acidity.

Pinot Blanc (white)

An easy-going and fruity grape offering good value, short-term wines in Alsace, Pinot Blanc is also found in Italy (as Pinot Bianco) and Austria, as Weissburgunder.

Which grapes are in the wines you know?

Below is a list of commonly found wines that provide no clues about the grapes that made them on the label. The list is ordered by country and region. The grapes noted are the main grapes used, local laws may allow additional varieties in the blends. You'll see that France is the major culprit for anonymity of grape variety. Elsewhere, the variety is very often mentioned on the label – in which case, it is not mentioned here.

France

Alsace

- Edelzwicker – blend of Alsace white grapes (which may include Riesling, Pinot Blanc, Pinot Gris, Muscat, Gewurztraminer, Sylvaner)

Beaujolais

All reds from Gamay, plus a very small number of whites from Chardonnay.

- St-Amour
- Chénas
- Régnié
- Moulin-à-Vent
- Fleurie
- Morgon

- Brouilly
- Côte de Brouilly
- Juliénas
- Chiroubles

Bordeaux

The appellations below comprise the following grape varieties: Cabernet Sauvignon, Merlot, Cabernet Franc, Petit Verdot (red), Sémillon, Sauvignon Blanc, Muscadelle (white).

- Côtes de Blaye
- Côtes de Bourg
- Côtes de Castillon
- Entre-Deux-Mers
- Fronsac
- Graves
- Haut-Médoc
- Lalande de Pomerol
- Listrac
- Loupiac
- Margaux
- Médoc
- Moulis
- Pauillac
- Pessac-Léognan
- Pomerol
- Premières Côtes de Blaye
- Premières Côtes de Bordeaux
- St-Emilion
- St-Estèphe
- St-Julien
- Ste-Croix-du-Mont
- Sauternes

Burgundy

Pinot Noir (red), Chardonnay (white) for all the following appellations.

- Beaune
- Chablis
- Chambolle-Musigny
- Chassagne-Montrachet

- Chevalier-Montrachet
- Côte de Beaune-Villages
- Côte de Nuits-Villages
- Fixin
- Gevrey-Chambertin
- Givry
- Mâcon
- Marsannay
- Mercurey
- Meursault
- Montagny
- Monthélie
- Morey-St-Denis
- Nuits-St-Georges
- Pernand-Vergelesses
- Pommard
- Pouilly-Fuissé
- Puligny-Montrachet
- Rully
- St-Aubin
- St-Romain
- St-Véran
- Santenay
- Savigny-lès-Beaune
- Volnay
- Vosne-Romanée
- Vougeot

Champagne

Chardonnay, Pinot Noir, Pinot Meunier.

- Blanc de blancs – Chardonnay
- Blanc de noirs – Pinot Noir and/or Pinot Meunier

Corsica

- Vin de Corse – Sciacarello, Nielluccio, Grenache, Syrah, Cinsault, Carignan, Barbarossa (red), Rolle, Trebbiano (white)

Jura

- Jura – Savagnin, Chardonnay (white)

Languedoc/Roussillon

- Banyuls – Grenache
- Corbières – Carignan, Syrah, Grenache, Mourvèdre, Cinsault, Terret Noir, Picpoul (red), Bourboulenc, Maccabeo, Roussanne, Muscat, Picpoul (white)
- Coteaux du Languedoc – Carignan, Syrah, Grenache, Mourvèdre, Lladoner Pelut, Cinsault, Terret, Counoise (red), Bourboulenc, Grenache Blanc, Clairette, Trebbiano, Picpoul, Roussanne, Marsanne, Rolle, Viognier (white)
- Côtes du Roussillon – Carignan, Syrah, Mourvèdre, Grenache, Cinsault, Lladoner Pelut (red), Maccabeo, Grenache Blanc, Roussanne, Marsanne, Rolle, Malvoisie (white)
- Faugères – Carignan, Syrah, Mourvèdre, Grenache, Lladoner Pelut, Cinsault (red)
- Fitou – Carignan, Grenache, Syrah, Mourvèdre, Lladoner Pelut, Cinsault (red)
- Maury – Grenache (red)
- Minervois – Carignan, Syrah, Grenache, Mourvèdre, Cinsault, Lladoner Pelut, (red, rosé), Bourboulenc, Maccabeo, Marsanne, Clairette, Grenache Blanc, Muscat
- St-Chinian – Carignan, Grenache, Mourvèdre, Syrah, Cinsault, Lladoner Pelut (red, rosé)

Loire Valley

- Anjou – Cabernet Franc, Cabernet Sauvignon, Gamay (red), Chenin Blanc, Sauvignon Blanc (white)
- Bonnezeaux – Chenin Blanc
- Chinon – Cabernet Franc (red), Chenin Blanc (white)
- Coteaux du Layon – Chenin Blanc
- Jasnières – Chenin Blanc (white)
- Menetou-Salon – Pinot Noir (red, rosé), Sauvignon Blanc (white)
- Montlouis – Chenin Blanc (white)
- Muscadet – Melon de Bourgogne (white)
- Pouilly-Fumé – Sauvignon Blanc (white
- Quincy – Sauvignon Blanc (white)
- St-Nicolas de Bourgueil – Cabernet Franc (red)
- Sancerre – Pinot Noir (red/rosé), Sauvignon Blanc (white)
- Saumur – Cabernet Franc (red), Chenin Blanc (white)
- Savennières – Chenin Blanc (white)

- Touraine – Gamay, Cabernet Franc, Pinot Noir, Grolleau (red, rosé), Chenin Blanc, Sauvignon Blanc (white)
- Vouvray – Chenin Blanc (white)

Provence

- Bandol – Mourvèdre, Grenache, Cinsault (red)
- Cassis – Mourvèdre, Cinsault, Grenache (red), Clairette, Marsanne, Trebbiano, Sauvignon Blanc, Bourboulenc (white)
- Coteaux d'Aix-en-Provence – Grenache, Carignan, Cinsault, Syrah, Mourvèdre, Cabernet Sauvignon, Counoise (red), Clairette, Sauvignon Blanc, Trebbiano, Sémillon, Grenache Blanc, Bourboulenc (white)
- Côtes de Provence – Carignan, Grenache, Mourvèdre, Tibouren, Cinsault, Syrah, Cabernet Sauvignon, (rosé, red), Sémillon, Clairette, Rolle, Trebbiano (white)

Rhône Valley

- Châteauneuf-du-Pape – Grenache, Syrah, Cinsault, Carignan, Mourvèdre, Gamay, Terret Noir, Counoise, Vaccarèse, Roussanne, Bourboulenc, Muscardin, Clairette, Picardin
- Condrieu – Viognier (white)
- Cornas – Syrah (red)
- Côte Rôtie – Syrah, Viognier (red)
- Coteaux du Tricastin – Grenache, Syrah, Cinsault, Mourvèdre, Carignan, Picpoul, Grenache Blanc, Clairette, Roussanne, Viognier, Marsanne, Trebbiano (red, white, rosé)
- Côtes du Lubéron – Grenache, Syrah, Mourvèdre, Cinsault, Carignan (red), Grenache Blanc, Clairette, Bourboulenc, Marsanne, Roussanne, Trebbiano (white)
- Côtes du Rhône and Côte du Rhône-Villages – Grenache, Syrah, Mourvèdre, Carignan, Cinsault, Picpoul Noir, Camarèse, Muscardin, Clairette Rosé (red, rosé), Grenache Blanc, Marsanne, Roussanne, Bourboulenc, Viognier, Clairette, Picpoul Blanc, Trebbiano (white)
- Côtes du Ventoux – Carignan, Grenache, Mourvèdre, Cinsault, Syrah, Picpoul, Counoise (red), Clairette, Bourboulenc (white)
- Crozes-Hermitage – Syrah (red), Marsanne, Roussane (white)
- Gigondas – Grenache, Syrah, Mourvèdre, Carignan, Cinsault (red, rosé)
- Hermitage – Syrah (red), Marsanne, Roussanne (white)
- Lirac – Grenache, Syrah, Mourvèdre, Cinsault, Carignan (red),

Clairette, Marsanne, Roussanne, Bourboulenc, Trebbiano (white)
- Rasteau – Grenache, Syrah, Carignan, Cinsault (red)
- St-Joseph – Syrah (red), Roussanne, Marsanne (white)
- St-Peray – Marsanne, Roussanne (white)
- Tavel – Grenache, Cinsault, Syrah, Carignan, Bourboulenc, Mourvèdre, Picpoul, Calitor (rosé)
- Vacqueyras – Grenache, Syrah, Mourvèdre, Cinsault, Carignan (red), Clairette, Grenache Blanc, Marsanne, Roussanne, Viognier, Bourboulenc (white)

Savoie
- Vin de Savoie – Gamay, Pinot Noir, Mondeuse (red), Chasselas, Aligoté, Roussanne (white)

South west
- Bergerac – Cabernet Sauvignon, Cabernet Franc, Merlot (red), Sauvignon Blanc, Sémillon, Muscadelle (white)
- Buzet – Merlot, Cabernet Sauvignon, Cabernet Franc, Malbec (red), Sauvignon Blanc, Sémillon, Muscadelle (white)
- Cahors – Malbec, Merlot, Tannat, Folle Noir (red)
- Côtes de Duras – Merlot, Cabernet Sauvignon, Cabernet Franc, Malbec (red), Sémillon, Sauvignon Blanc, Muscadelle (white)
- Côtes du Frontonnais – Négrette, Cabernet Franc, Cabernet Sauvignon, Syrah, Gamay, Tannat (red)
- Côtes du Marmandais – Cabernet Sauvignon, Cabernet Franc, Merlot, Malbec, Fer, Syrah, Abouriou (red), Sauvignon Blanc, Sémillon, Muscadelle (white)
- Irrouléguy – Tannat, Cabernet Sauvignon, Cabernet Franc (red, rosé), Gros Manseng, Petit Manseng, Petit Courbu (white)
- Jurançon – Gros Manseng, Petit Manseng (white)
- Madiran – Tannat, Cabernet Sauvignon, Cabernet Franc, Fer (red)
- Monbazillac – Sauvignon Blanc, Sémillon, Muscadelle (white)
- Pacherenc du Vic Bilh – Arrufiac, Courbu, Petit Manseng, Gros Manseng, Sauvignon Blanc (white)
- Pécharmant – Merlot, Cabernet Sauvignon, Cabernet Franc, Malbec (red)

Italy

Campania
- Taurasi – Aglianico (red)

Friuli-Venezia Giulia
- Collio – Ribollo Gialla, Malvasia, Tocai Friulano (white)
- Friuli Isonzo – Merlot, Cabernet Franc, Cabernet Sauvignon, Refosco, Pinot Noir (red), Tocai Friulano, Malvasia, Pinot Blanc, Chardonnay (white)

Latium
- Castelli Romani – Cesanesi, Merlot, Sangiovese, Montepulciano, Nero Buono (red), Malvasia, Trebbiano (white)
- Colli Albani – Malvasia, Trebbiano (white)
- Frascati – Malvasia, Trebbiano, Greco (white)

Liguria
- Cinque Terre – Bosco, Albarola, Vermentino (white)

Lombardy
- Franciacorta – Pinot Noir, Pinot Blanc, Chardonnay (rosé, white)
- Oltrepò Pavese – Barbera, Uva Rara, Ughetta, Croatina, Pinot Noir (red)
- Valtellina – Nebbiolo (red)

Marche
- Rosso Conero – Montepulciano (red)
- Rosso Piceno – Sangiovese, Montepulciano (red)

Molise
- Molise – Montepulciano (red), Chardonnay, Pinot Blanc, Moscato (white)

Piedmont
- Barbaresco – Nebbiolo (red)
- Barolo – Nebbiolo (red)
- Gattinara – Nebbiolo (red)
- Gavi di Gavi – Cortese (white)
- Roero – Nebbiolo (red), Arneis (white)

Puglia
- Copertino – Negroamaro, Malvasia, Sangiovese (red, rosé)
- Salice Salentino – Negroamaro (red)

Sicily

- Cerasulo di Vittoria – Nero d'Avola, Frappato (red)
- Marsala – Grillo, Catarratto, Inzolia, Damaschino, Pignatello, Calabrese, Nerello Mascalese, Nero d'Avola (red, white)

Trentino-Alto-Adige

- Trentino – Cabernet Sauvignon, Merlot (red), Chardonnay, Pinot Blanc (white)

Tuscany

- Bolgheri – Sangiovese, Canaiolo, Cabernet Sauvignon, Merlot (red)
- Bolgheri-Sassicaia – Cabernet Sauvigon, Sangiovese (red)
- Brunello di Montalcino – Sangiovese (red)
- Carmignano – Sangiovese, Canaiolo, Cabernet Sauvignon, Cabernet Franc, Trebbiano, Malvasia (red, rosé)
- Chianti – Sangiovese, Canaiolo (red)
- Vino Nobile di Montepulciano – Sangiovese (red)

Umbria

- Orvieto – Trebbiano, Verdello, Grechetto, Malvasia, Canaiolo Bianco (white)

Veneto

- Amarone della Valpolicella – Corvina, Rondinella, Molinara (red)
- Bardolino – Corvina, Rondinella, Molinara, Negrara (red)
- Bianco di Custoza – Trebbiano, Garganega, Tocai Friulano, Cortese, Malvasia, Welschriesling, Chardonnay (white)
- Soave – Garganega, Trebbiano (white)
- Valpolicella – Corvina, Rondinella, Molinara (red)

Spain

Andalucía

- Jerez-Xérès-Sherry – Palomino, Muscat (white)

Aragón

- Calatayud – Grenache, Tempranillo, Carignan, Merlot, Cabernet Sauvignon, Syrah (red), Macabeo, Malvasia, Chardonnay, Muscat, Grenache Blanc (white)

- Somontano – Grenache, Cabernet Sauvignon, Moristel, Parellada, Tempranillo, Merlot, Pinot Noir, Syrah (red), Grenache Blanc, Chardonnay, Alcañon, Macabeo (white)
- Campo de Borja – Grenache, Cabernet Sauvignon, Carignan, Tempranillo (red)

Catalonia

- Alella – Tempranillo, Grenache (red), Pansa Blanca, Grenache Blanc (white)
- Penedès – Cabernet Sauvignon, Grenache, Carignan, Mourvèdre, Ull de Liebre (red), Macabeo, Parellada, Xarel-lo (white)
- Priorato – Grenache, Carignan, Cabernet Sauvignon, Merlot, Syrah (red), Grenache Blanc, Macabeo, Pedro Ximénez, Chardonnay (white)

Castilla-La Mancha

- La Mancha – Tempranillo, Cabernet Sauvignon, Grenache, Merlot, Moravia (red), Airén, Macabeo, Pardilla

Castilla y León

- Bierzo – Grenache, Mencia (red)
- Ribera del Duero – Tempranillo, Grenache, Cabernet Sauvignon, Merlot (red)
- Rueda – Verdejo, Sauvignon Blanc (white)
- Toro – Tempranillo, Grenache (red)

Cava

From several regions: Xarel-lo, Macabeo, Parellada, Chardonnay (white)

La Rioja

- Rioja – Tempranillo, Grenache, Graciano, Carignan, Cabernet Sauvignon (red), Macabeo, Grenache Blanc, Malvasia (white)

Málaga

- Pedro Ximénez, Moscatel (white)

Murcia

- Bullas – Mourvèdre, Tempranillo (red)
- Jumilla – Mourvèdre, Cabernet Sauvignon, Tempranillo, Grenache, Merlot (red), Airén, Macabeo, Pedro Ximénez (white)

Navarra

- Navarra – Cabernet Sauvignon, Grenache, Graciano, Merlot, Carignan, Tempranillo (red), Grenache Blanc, Chardonnay, Malvasia, Moscatel, Macabeo (white)

Valencia

- Valencia – Grenache, Mourvèdre, Tempranillo, Tintorera, Bodal, Cabernet Sauvignon, Forcallat (red, rosé), Macabeo, Malvasia, Merseguera, Muscat, Pedro Ximénez, Planta Fina de Pedralba, Planta Nova, Tortosi, Verdil (white)

Portugal

Alentejano

- Alentejo – Tempranillo, Periquita, Trincadeira (red), Antao Vaz, Arinto, Perrum, Siria (white)

Beiras

- Bairrada – Baga, Bastardo, Camarate, Jaen (red, rosé), Arinto, Bical (white)
- Dão – Touriga Nacional, Alfrocheiro Preto, Bastardo, Jaen, Tempranillo, Tinta Pinheira (red, rosé), Encruzado, Assario Branco, Barcelo, Bical, Cerceal, Verdelho (white)

Madeira

- Madeira – Tinta Negra Mole, Boal, Sercial, Verdelho, Malvasia

Minho

- Vinho Verde – Loureiro, Alvarinho (white)

Ribatejano

- Ribatejo – Baga, Camarate, Trincadeira, Perequita (red, rosé), Arinto, Fernão Pires, Trebbiano, Trincadeira das Pratas (white)

Trás-os-Montes

- Douro – Touriga Nacional, Touriga Francesa, Tempranillo, Tinto Barroca, Tinta Cão, Tinta Amarela, Tinta Pinheira, Alfrocheiro Preto, Jaen, Mourisco Tinto, Bastardo (red), Encruzado, Verdelho, Viosinho, Rabigato, Malvasia Fina, Donzelinho, Douro Superior
- Port – Touriga Nacional, Touriga Francesa, Tinta Cão, Tempranillo, Tinta Barroca (red)

04

climate and place

In this chapter you will learn:
- how climate and place affect the flavours of wine
- the relative importance of the different elements of climate
- the difference in taste between warm- and cool-climate wines
- how climate change is affecting wine
- the meaning of *terroir* – and whether or not you can really taste it.

One of the things you hear the most when visiting wineries these days is that wine is made in the vineyard. This doesn't mean that winemakers are moving their fermentation tanks into the fields. It's just that they recognize that it is the quality of fruit that is the principal determinant of the quality of the wine, rather than anything that happens in the winery. It is almost impossible to make a good wine from bad grapes. And to make great wine, top-quality grapes are essential.

The quality of grapes depends largely on where in the world they are grown. The most important deciding factor on where to grow grapes is the prevailing climate. Other factors to consider will be the type of soil and other specifics of the vineyard site. In this chapter, you will learn how the place the grapes are grown will influence a wine's type and range of flavours.

Climate: what difference does it really make?

The quality and style of any wine is intimately linked to the temperature and available water during the grapes' growing season. Climate differs from weather in that the former refers to the general growing conditions, whereas the latter refers to the specific conditions in a given year, or vintage.

Climate makes all the difference in the world to wine. It is the single most important element in determining wine quality. Like all plants, the vine has basic minimum requirements for sunlight, warmth and moisture to survive. Wine-growing regions are usually situated in two bands around the globe, 30° to 50° north and south of the equator, although with modern advances in viticulture and changes in climate, grape growers are pushing the boundaries of climate outside these zones. Vines can now be found in such unlikely places as Thailand, India and Ethiopia, and the northerly English vineyards are producing sparkling wine good enough to tempt French Champagne houses to invest in *les vins anglais*.

Did you know?

The Vale do São Francisco tropical vineyards of Brazil are 9° from the equator and produce two grape harvests every year.

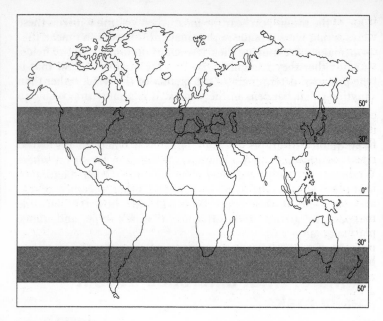

figure 4.1 wine-growing regions are generally situated 30° to 50° north and south of the equator

Grapevines are not fussy plants and will thrive in dry, stony soil that is considered unsuitable for other crops. In fact, it is often the case that the more inhospitable the terrain, the more promising the location for wine grapes. To produce fruit that is suitable for making into wine, the climate should be moderately warm: if it is too hot the grapes will taste baked; too cold and they will fail to ripen sufficiently and taste green and acidic.

In warmer climates, fruit will ripen reliably and quickly. These are the growing conditions that prevail in many parts of the new world and southern Europe. In these climates there is rarely any question of whether or not the grapes will ripen, although there will be differences in weather from one year to the next that will influence the quality of the vintage, for example spring frosts, summer hailstorms and other extreme weather events. Where grapes are guaranteed to ripen fully, though, there will be less vintage variation than in cooler climates. There will also be an abundance of ripe fruit flavours in the wine. This ripeness of flavour has great appeal and explains the popularity of wines from more reliably warm countries such as Australia. Since variations in weather can often have a negative influence on wine quality in the traditional regions of northern Europe, it's no surprise that people often choose to buy a new world bottle in the knowledge that it will taste more or less the same every year.

You might think that the hotter the climate, the better the conditions for growing grapes. This is not the case. The longer it takes grapes to ripen, the more interesting and complex their flavours (and those in the wine) are likely to be. Grapes that ripen too quickly are likely to be low in flavour and aroma. While it is certainly easier and usually cheaper to make a wine in a place with a reliable and hot climate, the most interesting and sought-after wines tend to come from climates that are marginal for the varieties of grapes that are grown. In these places, grapes only just ripen successfully – and even then, perhaps not every year. Think of the difference in flavour between strawberries grown in England and Spain. A naturally ripe English strawberry, if you can find one, will have more aroma and a finer flavour than one that has quickly ripened in the hotter Spanish sun.

Different grape varieties bud and ripen at different times, so climate is a fundamental consideration for grape growers when they are deciding what can and should be planted. Cabernet Sauvignon ripens more slowly than Pinot Noir, for example, which means Cabernet needs to be planted in a climate that remains warm through the end of summer and into the autumn, otherwise the grapes will never ripen. Pinot Noir, on the other hand, is better suited to cooler climates because although the grapes will ripen easily in a warm climate, they will not achieve any complexity of flavour. They will also lose their fresh acidity rapidly if the weather is too warm at the end of the season.

Riesling is another grape variety that needs to ripen slowly if it is to develop the unique and interesting characteristics for which it is valued, but, unlike Pinot Noir, Riesling grapes can be left on the vine late in the season and still retain their typically crisp acidity. Grapes destined for sweet Riesling styles can be left in the vineyard for months after other grapes have been harvested, just as long as the weather remains fine.

Most grape growers will try to maximize the natural conditions they have in order to produce good quality wines within the confines of their climate. In every climate, there will always be some grapes that are an easy choice and others that are more of a challenge. In South Africa the most-planted variety is Chenin Blanc. This is not the most popular grape variety internationally (which is why much of it is now being pulled up to plant grapes that are more fashionable). But one major advantage of planting Chenin Blanc in a hotter area is that it always retains good levels of acidity, even if the climate is very warm, and acidity is important to create a balanced wine that is refreshing to drink.

Another factor influencing choice of grape variety is that some varieties are more tolerant of extremes of climate than others. Some varieties resist drought and the effects of high rainfall better than others. Some varieties have a narrow picking window, which is another consideration influencing the decision to plant them. The quality of Syrah (Shiraz) grapes will deteriorate quickly if the grapes are not picked when they are ready. Other varieties – Cabernet Sauvignon, for example – are far more resistant to longer 'hang-time', so that even if the flavour profile of the grapes changes, good wine can still be made. Climate is most important for grapes that ripen relatively early or relatively late, since it is for these varieties that the risk of overripening or underripening is the greatest.

Key elements of climate

Temperature, sunlight and rainfall – as well as humidity and wind – will all affect how grapes ripen and how the resulting wine will taste.

Temperature

The most important basic element for grape growing, as for any fruit culture, is temperature. A prolonged period of summer warmth is needed to ripen wine grapes. The vine's shoots start to grow at around 10°C and flowering takes place at 15°C–20°C. Thereafter, average temperatures of 15°C–30°C are needed to sustain the plant's photosynthesis. At temperatures higher than this, the vine will start to suffer from heat stress and may cease to ripen its fruit. There should ideally be a significant difference between summer and winter temperatures to allow the vine a period of dormancy, although at very low temperatures (below about -15°C), vines may not survive the winter.

The effects of temperature can be managed by selecting vineyard sites at differing altitudes. Average temperature falls around

0.5°C for every 100 metres of altitude, so the growing conditions of the vine can be substantially altered by altitude. How temperature changes between day and night also has a great effect on how grapes ripen, particularly in hot climates. If the temperature around the vine (and in the soil) is unremittingly hot day and night, the grapes will lack acidity and wines made from these grapes are liable to taste flat, stewed or baked. On the other hand, if hot daytime temperatures are balanced with cold nights (as is usually the case at higher altitudes, or in coastal regions, or in mountainous regions), the grapes will have better balance, and retain the acidity they need to make good wine.

How temperature affects where grapes can grow

The table on page 62 shows the flexibility of different grape varieties to grow within different temperature bands, and therefore why various grape varieties are suited to different climates. You will see that Pinot Noir has a very limited range of growing temperatures within which successful wine can be made, which explains its relative scarcity and high prices. The climate-maturity groupings shown below are based on the relationship between growing requirements and climate for premium wine production in the world's benchmark regions for each grape variety. NH and SH refer to northern hemisphere and southern hemisphere. The chart is a work in progress of Dr Gregory V. Jones, of Southern Oregon University.

Sunlight

Essential for all plants for photosynthesis, sunlight is a natural element that is carefully monitored by grape growers, in all types of climate. The vine is a climbing plant that was traditionally grown high on pergola trellises. But this training system shades the grapes, which makes them ripen more slowly (some may not even ripen at all). Modern vine growing focuses more on managing the grapes' exposure to sunlight in order to achieve consistent and complete ripeness within the constraints of the usual weather patterns. Grape growers will consider factors such as the orientation of their vineyard and rows of vines within it, how far apart to space the vines and the rows, training the plants onto wires or posts, and pruning the leaf area to give the grapes greater or reduced exposure to sunlight. These decisions will depend on the grape varieties grown, since their growing patterns and vigour vary.

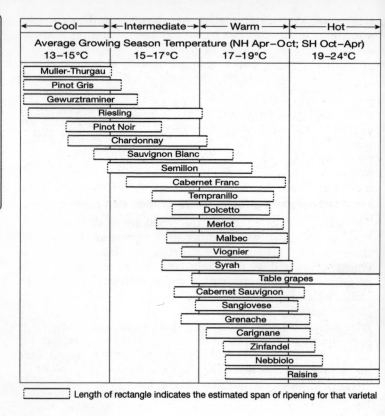

◄——Cool——►	◄—Intermediate—►	◄——Warm——►	◄——Hot——►
Average Growing Season Temperature (NH Apr–Oct; SH Oct–Apr)			
13–15°C	15–17°C	17–19°C	19–24°C

Muller-Thurgau
Pinot Gris
Gewurztraminer
Riesling
Pinot Noir
Chardonnay
Sauvignon Blanc
Semillon
Cabernet Franc
Tempranillo
Dolcetto
Merlot
Malbec
Viognier
Syrah
Table grapes
Cabernet Sauvignon
Sangiovese
Grenache
Carignane
Zinfandel
Nebbiolo
Raisins

Length of rectangle indicates the estimated span of ripening for that varietal

figure 4.2 grapevine climate/maturity groupings

Grapes grown at high altitude have greater exposure to ultraviolet radiation, and they produce more vivid and deeply coloured red wines.

Try this

Try an Argentinian Malbec from the high-altitude vineyards of Tupungato, in Mendoza, to see how the naturally purple colour of the Malbec is especially vibrant from these high sites.

High ultraviolet radiation is a feature of the vineyards of Central Otago in southern New Zealand, due to the thinner ozone layer here. The unique quality of the light and how it reflects off the soil and onto the grapes contributes to the distinctive character of this region's delicious Pinot Noir wines.

White wine grapes react less positively than red wine grapes to ultraviolet radiation. Researchers at Germany's Geisenheim viticultural research institute controlled the exposure of white grapes to ultraviolet radiation and conducted taste trials on the wines made from the grapes. They concluded that high levels of ultraviolet radiation were detrimental to the quality of the wines. Their findings showed that people initially preferred the wines with high ultraviolet radiation exposure, as the wines were more tropical and fruity. But over quite a short period, these wines were found to age less well than white wines with lower levels of ultraviolet exposure. This probably explains why there are very few age-worthy white wines grown in the very sunniest parts of the globe.

Rainfall

High or low rainfall is not the issue when growing vines: it's when it falls that matters. Rain in winter does nothing more than build water reserves. Rain in the early part of the growing season can be detrimental to the size of the crop by affecting flowering and fruit set. Later on, heavy rainfall and humidity can lead to a range of fungal diseases that, if left untreated, will greatly diminish or even destroy the crop. Rain in the month or two before harvest has the greatest impact on wine quality. There is a saying in France: 'août fait le moût', meaning 'August makes the must'. This is the time when grapes need to be concentrating their flavours to achieve the perfect balance between richness of flavour and ripe fruit acids. Excess water at this stage can result in wines with dilute flavours and, if rot sets in, off flavours may also be detectable in the wine if the grapes are not carefully sorted.

Rot is the most feared consequence of rain. It can quickly spread through a vineyard, devastating the crop. For winemakers in the many regions of the world where autumn rain is bound to arrive sooner or later, deciding when to harvest the grapes is a nail-biting gamble against the weather. Grape growers need to balance their desire for ripe flavours in their wines against the risks of rain and rot damaging their precious, once-a-year opportunity to make the best wine they can.

Try these

Find two Bordeaux red wines (ideally from the same producer) from the 2007 and 2005 vintages, and compare the two. You will see the difference rainfall can make to wine. 2005 was a great vintage; 2007 suffered a very rainy summer. The result? 2007 wines taste lighter and less concentrated in flavour. Some taste green and underripe, because the grapes didn't get enough sunshine to finish ripening. 2005 wines are more concentrated and balanced, which means they will age better and more slowly than the 2007 wines.

In places where summer rainfall is minimal or absent (parts of Australia, California and Chile, for example), growers have fewer worries at harvest time, but need to compensate for the lack of water during the growing season by irrigation. The way a vine is irrigated will affect the quality of the grapes in the same way that rainfall can. Sometimes irrigation techniques attempt to replicate the weather, with periodic flooding of the vineyards. For better quality wines, the most common practice is drip irrigation, which gives the vines a controlled, low dose of water as needed.

When hot can be cool: macroclimate and microclimate

The difference between macroclimate and microclimate is important, as it can mean the difference between good and bad wine, or determine whether grapes can be grown at all. The microclimate of a vine is the climate in its immediate surroundings, whereas the macroclimate includes the wider area. The microclimate can vary from the broader macroclimate because of factors such as the altitude of the vineyard, the direction the vines face, or the influence of geographical features such as mountains, lakes or oceans. There can be several different microclimates within a single, small plot of vines.

In cooler climates, vine growers tend to make use of microclimates to make growing conditions warmer, whereas in hotter climates the reverse is the case. This is why you will notice some wine back labels telling you that the vineyards are cool whereas others may want their customers to know that the vineyard is warm and sunny. For example, in Burgundy's cool, frost-prone climate most of the best sites for growing grapes are to be found on the warmer, south-east-facing slopes at an altitude of between 250 to 350 metres above sea level, where the climatic conditions are most favourable. Similarly, in the cool, northerly Mosel Valley in Germany, vines are planted on vertiginous slopes on the winding bends in the river because this ensures maximum exposure to the sun.

In hot climates, growers may plant at higher altitudes to moderate the effects of the climate: in Argentina, Malbec grown at high altitudes often produces the best quality wine, with more natural crispness and freshness of flavour. Conversely, in Chile and the United States, vines grown on flat land near the Pacific coast will experience cooler conditions than some inland slopes, due to the influence of the cool air coming from the ocean. In South Africa viticulture is only possible at all thanks to the cold ocean currents that sweep up from Antarctica.

Did you know?

Red wines from high-altitude vineyards may be better for your health. The especially high levels of ultraviolet light stimulate production of healthy polyphenols in the grapes.

Try these

Buy two Sauvignon Blanc wines from Chile. If possible, try to find wines made by the same producer. Buy one from Casablanca Valley and one from Leyda Valley. Casablanca Valley is close to the coast, but Leyda Valley is even closer. This extra proximity to the ocean gives the Leyda wines added crispness and herbaceous vitality. You could also try a third wine, from further inland, in the Central Valley. Here, the warmer climate produces wines with riper, more tropical flavours and less obvious freshness.

Tasting the effect of climate

Understanding the climate of a wine region will give you a pretty good idea of the style of wine you can expect to find in the bottle. The table below gives examples of how the climate of a region influences the characteristics of the wines in different parts of the world. This is not intended to be a definitive list, as the effects of climate can be moderated by an individual

Wine characteristics by climate type

Climate	Wine characteristics	Regions
Very cool, marginal for most grape growing	• far more white than red wines • ideal for sparkling wines • some high-quality whites • most red varieties, hard to ripen • high acidity, wines always taste fresh; less ripe wines can taste green • often strongly aromatic (if aromatic grape varieties are used) • light in colour • light-bodied • lower levels of alcohol • significant vintage variation	*England* *France* – Chablis, Champagne, Savoie *Germany* – Mosel, Rheingau *Portugal* – Minho (Vinho Verde) *Canada* *USA* – New York Finger Lakes
Cool, can be hard to ripen some varieties	• more white than red wines • wide range of whites • limited number of reds • more white than red wines • often strongly aromatic • many high-quality whites • fewer (though notable) high-quality reds • light- to medium-weight • crisp acidity • noticeable tannins • usually moderate alcohol • significant vintage variation	*France* – Alsace, Burgundy, Loire Valley, Beaujolais *Italy* – Alto Adige, Friuli *Spain* – Rías Baixas *Austria* *Switzerland* *Germany* – Rheinhessen, Pfalz, Franken, Baden *Hungary* *Slovenia* *Chile* – coastal *South Africa* – coastal *USA* – Oregon, Carneros *Australia* – Tasmania, Yarra Valley, Adelaide Hills *New Zealand*

Warm, but variations in weather can impede ripening	• wide range of reds and whites • medium-bodied • vintage variation more marked for reds than for whites, since whites ripen at cooler temperatures • balanced acidity • moderately aromatic • firm tannins • moderate alcohol • high-quality reds and whites	*France* – Bordeaux, south west, northern Rhône *Spain* – Rioja, Ribera del Duero *Italy* – Veneto, Piedmont, Tuscany *Portugal* – Bairrada, Dão *USA* – Washington State
Reliably warm, grapes usually ripen well	• more red than white wines • more regular vintages for reds and whites • riper and sweeter fruit flavours • moderate to high alcohol • lower levels of natural acidity • smoother tannins • full-bodied whites • medium- to full-bodied reds • can be high quality, mainly for reds	*France* – southern Rhône, Languedoc-Roussillon Most of *Spain* *Greece* *Bulgaria* *South Africa* *Chile* *Argentina* *USA* – northern California (Napa Valley) *Australia* – Clare Valley, Coonawarra, Western Australia
Very warm, grapes ripen easily	• more red than white wines • very ripe fruit, sometimes overripe and raisined • low levels of acidity, so wines taste richer • less vintage variation • higher alcohol • softer tannins • full-bodied • some high-quality red wines in fuller, riper styles • lighter styles possible from early-picked grapes	*Italy* – south *Portugal* – south (Alentejo), Douro Valley *Australia* – Barossa Valley, Hunter Valley, McLaren Vale *Spain* – south (Jerez) *USA* – Central Valley, California

vineyard's altitude, aspect and proximity to water, among other things. Furthermore, as you will see in the following chapter, the winemaker can also influence the style of wines produced in spite of the climate, as is the case in the light and elegant white wines produced from Australia's hot Hunter Valley. There are fewer options available for a winemaker operating in a very cool climate, or a climate that is marginal for the grape variety he or she is trying to grow.

Climate change: how does it affect the wines you drink?

Climate change is not a future concern: it has already happened. Average temperatures have risen throughout the world in the past 50 years, and the effects of this can already be seen in riper grapes and riper flavours in some wines. Average alcohol levels have risen as the combined result of higher sugar levels in grapes and the fashion for wines that are fruity and easy to enjoy young. The effects are most significant in Europe, where in the past vintages in cooler regions were more irregular than they are today. Now, grapes ripen more reliably, and earlier, and picking dates have moved forward. The harvest in Châteauneuf-du-Pape, in the southern Rhône region of France, for example, now takes place a full month earlier than it did in 1945.

So far, climate change has been good for wine lovers, as it means there are more places in the world that can produce good quality wines. But the disadvantages of climate change are becoming clear. As you can surmise from Dr Jones's table, earlier in this chapter, if average temperatures in the hotter growing regions of the world rise by just a couple of degrees Celsius (as is predicted to happen over the next 50 years), growing wine grapes may no longer be viable. Even in cooler areas, an increase in temperatures will radically affect the grapes that can be successfully grown.

It might be that the world's most famous regions suffer the most, as their reputations have been built on hundreds of years of a stable climate. Generations of winemakers have established that these climates are perfect for producing particular grapes: Cabernet Sauvignon in Bordeaux, and Pinot Noir in Burgundy, for example. It is likely that the most highly regarded vineyard locations today will cease to be quality leaders for the rest of the world. One leading viticulturist suggested in early 2008 that Bordeaux may have already had its best vintages for Cabernet Sauvignon.

Water availability is a major issue. If Australia's drought continues, it will become uneconomic to produce high-volume wines from the hot, irrigated inland areas, and there will certainly be more pressing concerns for water use than growing grapes to make wine. It is likely that the Australian wine industry will become more focused on niche production of high-end wines, which do not require irrigation, or where the price of the wine can justify the high costs of production. Elsewhere, such as in parts of Spain, growers are already exploring vineyard sites at higher altitude, to benefit from cooler growing conditions.

An especially worrying feature of climate change for winemakers is that there is predicted to be an increase in the occurrence of the freakish weather events we have seen in the past few years, such as floods, droughts, hailstorms and heatwaves. Any event that cannot be planned for is likely to have detrimental effects on grape growing and the quality of wine.

Of course, where some areas lose out, others will benefit. Marginal grape growing regions like England are enjoying far better conditions for viticulture as a result of higher temperatures. But for a vineyard owner today, planning for the future has probably never been more difficult. Not only do growers need to predict future demand, they also need to try to work out how changes in climate will influence the ripening of their grapes. Unlike other crops, grapevines do not deliver grapes that can be used for wine until several years have elapsed (usually three). And the quality of fruit the vine produces will usually improve over the years. For many good wines, the average age of the vines producing the fruit is 20 years or more.

These changes in growing conditions will mean that climate will assume an even greater importance as a factor influencing the styles of wine we drink. In the near future, you can expect to see a continued increase in riper, fruitier wines with higher levels of alcohol. Soon, it is likely that there will be changes in the varieties that are planted by region and the styles of wine made as winemakers adapt to changes in climate.

Terroir: the importance of place

Did you know?

Those confusing French wine labels covered with place names are all about *terroir*.

This French term, with no direct English translation, is the Holy Grail of viticulture or pure marketing hogwash, depending on whom you talk to. The former view tends to be espoused by people making wine in France, the latter by new world winemakers (especially outspoken Australians). But although it is a French word, *terroir* is a global concept. Most people have a view that falls somewhere in between the two extremes, acknowledging the existence of *terroir*, but divided as to its importance and precise definition. The only thing about *terroir* that nobody disputes is that it is a very controversial subject. So what is it?

In France, the term is often equated with 'soil', but there is a lot more to *terroir* than this. *Terroir* can be defined as the growing conditions of a particular site that differentiate it from anywhere else. It is the essence of place. Every vineyard (even a bad one) can be said to have its own, unique *terroir*. There are different definitions of the term, but *terroir* can include the climate, the soil, the grape variety, the site (the slope and orientation of the vineyard, and so on), and the influence of the hand of Man. The latter could be anything from the way the vines are trained to the decision on when to pick the grapes.

So, can you taste *terroir* in a wine? Some say never, and some say always. The term is often used as a symbol of the mysticism of wine, to signify the value of the exact spot where the vines were grown and to add value to a wine. Look at the marketing value of place to a wine brand. Consider how many wine producers associate their brand with a (possibly fictitious) 'creek', 'hill', or 'river' to imbue the wine with an all-important sense of place. If where wine comes from matters to you – and for most of us it does – then *terroir* is something you care about.

For a wine that is made from a blend of grapes coming from diverse vineyards that may be hundreds of kilometres apart, it's hard to argue that there is any meaningful *terroir* influence in the wine. For a small vineyard that produces wine with an identifiable style, year in, year out, most people would agree that the *terroir* does influence the wine. The argument is more forceful in a region like Burgundy, where several growers may produce wine from a site that clearly speaks of its origins, despite being made by different people.

It can be surprising just how different from each other two wines that have been made from the same grape variety, by the same person, at the same time, can taste, where the only difference is that the grapes were grown in plots 100 metres apart. This is the reason a producer in one small area might have many different wines, each one a bottled embodiment of a place. From one small village to the next, the difference in style and taste of wines can be remarkable.

Try these

Taste two Burgundy red wines (preferably from the same year), one from Pommard and the other from Volnay. Notice how different they taste. Volnay wines are fragrant, floral and delicate; Pommard wines are firm, with noticeable minerality and tannins. They are both made wholly from the Pinot Noir grape. Now look on a map and see just how close those two neighbouring villages are. The difference in taste is explained by the influence of *terroir*.

A further point to remember about *terroir* is that it can be good or bad. If one part of the globe makes consistently poor wine, year in and year out, it just doesn't have good *terroir* to produce wine.

05

the winemaker

In this chapter you will learn:
- how the person who makes the wine influences its flavour
- how to recognize oak in a wine (and whether you like it)
- how to identify the style of a wine before you open the bottle
- how red, white, sparkling, sweet and fortified wines are made.

You probably don't care how the oranges in a carton of juice were processed, nor who was responsible for making it. But with wine, these things matter. With wine, people matter. The third important variable influencing the flavours of wine, along with the grape variety and the place, is the human element. If a wine can be said to have personality, this is as much a reflection of the person who made it as it is of the ground where the grapes were grown. The winemaker's decisions can alter the nature of a wine completely. If you understand the different choices that have been made in the vineyard and winery you will be in a much better position to understand your own preferences for different styles of wine. This chapter looks at the human elements that affect the flavours in wine.

Choosing the fruit

The quality of fruit is crucial to the style and quality of wine. Fruit quality revolves around two factors: grape health and ripeness. The grape varieties used to make the wine are key to a wine's structure and flavour profile, as described in Chapter 03. The great majority of wines in the world are made from fresh, healthy, ripe grapes. But there are other options available to some winemakers.

Depending on the climatic conditions and regulations in the region, a winemaker may have free rein to use any grape varieties he or she chooses, as is the case in most parts of the New World, or may have to abide by local laws, as is the case in most parts of Europe. In Europe, wines that are defined by where they come from (by appellation or denomination of origin) are strictly controlled in terms of the grape varieties that may be used to make them. Generally speaking, the more prestigious the regional appellation, the more restrictive the laws governing which grapes may be used. For example, red wine appellations from the northern Rhône allow only one red grape, Syrah. And any white wine from the top Burgundy appellations in France can only be made with Chardonnay grapes.

The most important decision: when to pick

The exact ripeness of the grapes will determine the flavours in the wine. In the past, the ripeness of grapes was judged according to the amount of sugar in the berries (known as sugar ripeness). The quantity of sugar in the grapes directly affects the amount of alcohol in the wine made from them. European wine law regulates minimum natural sugar levels in grapes, and whether extra sugar may be added to the fermentation tank to increase the level of alcohol in a wine. But while sugar ripeness is still the key measure used to ascertain the potential alcohol in grapes, winemakers increasingly focus on the ripeness of the whole berry, which includes the skins and the seeds. This is a less precise or objective measure, and it usually involves the winemaker tasting the grapes on the vine to decide if, in his or her view, they are ready to be picked. Grapes can attain sugar ripeness some time before they are considered fully, phenologically ripe, so there is a large degree of individual choice on the part of the wine producer regarding picking dates.

Some winemakers will choose to leave their grapes as long as possible on the vine before picking them (as has been the fashion in some parts of California in recent years). Or, they may choose to pick some or all of their grapes before they are fully ripe, or to pick and then dry them, or leave them to dessicate on the vine, or, in some cases, leave them to be affected by noble rot, to produce sweet wines. In rare instances they may even leave the grapes on the vines all winter to freeze, when they can make ice wine. Tiny quantities of this expensive wine are made, notably in Germany and Canada.

Picking grapes early is less common today than it was in the past, as tastes have changed in favour of riper flavours to produce wines that are immediately ready to drink. In cool climate regions, picking grapes early is often a way of being sure to avoid a crop spoiled by rain, but the trade-off is wine that may have unpalatable, unripe flavours.

In warmer parts of the world, it can be advantageous to pick at least some of a crop early. Sauvignon Blanc, grown in a warmer part of Chile, for example, can achieve better flavour and higher natural acidity if a portion of the crop is picked before it is fully ripe. For varieties where ripening is uneven, such as Zinfandel, picking while some of the grapes are not quite ripe is considered by some producers a necessity to create a balanced wine. The alternative of waiting until all of the grapes ripen would leave the earlier ripening grapes raisined and overripe. Others, though, are happy to do this, preferring to create a wine that has a more raisined style and a higher level of alcohol.

Grapes that are picked with less ripeness, and therefore, less sugar, will produce wines with lower levels of alcohol. This can be desirable in a hot climate, where alcohol levels may be higher than one would wish for a wine to be in balance. Producers may pick early to make a particular style of wine. In Australia's hot Hunter Valley, early-picked Sémillon grapes make some of the country's most distinctive, age-worthy and historic wines, at remarkably low levels of alcohol (around 11 per cent). In the cool and humid northern Portugese region of Vinho Verde, producers have another reason to pick early: here, regulations governing maximum alcohol levels mean that producers will be denied the appellation if their wines are over 13 per cent alcohol.

Often, winegrowers trying to produce sweet wines will pick grapes over several weeks, or even months, to achieve the optimal level of maturity. This is a work of dedication and it makes for a far more expensive harvest than for regular dry red or white wine, which is one of the reasons these wines tend to be more expensive. These practices are also risky: there is the ever-present danger of rot, plus the possible damage to the crop from insects and other pests. Furthermore, the volume of wine that can be produced is greatly reduced, so it needs to be special to outweigh the risks. The reward for successful winemakers, however, is wines with extra dimensions of concentration, strength and sweetness that can command prices high enough to justify the work required to produce them.

Try these

To see the effects of harvest timing on wines, try these:

- From early-picked grapes: Hunter Valley Sémillon, from Australia
- Sweet wines from nobly rotted grapes: Sauternes from Bordeaux, Tokaj Aszú from Hungary, Austrian sweet wines from the Neusiedlersee, or German wines labelled Beerenauslese or Trockenbeerenauslese
- From dried grapes: Amarone della Valpolicella, from Piedmont (a dry red), Vin Santo from Tuscany, or Vin de Paille from France.

Fermenting the grapes

Once the winemaker has chosen which grape varieties to use and when to pick them, the next decision is how to ferment the grapes. The basic fermentation process is the same for red and white wines, but white grapes are usually fermented without their skins. To make white wine fresh grapes are gently pressed to release their juice and the juice is removed from the skins. The juice may be left in a cool and protected environment for the solids to settle for a day or so before it is put into tanks or barrels to ferment. The basic method of making red wine involves light crushing of the grapes to break the berries, before they are transferred into a tank to ferment.

At ambient temperatures, yeasts will soon start to feed on the sugars in the grapes. As the wine ferments, these sugars are transformed into alcohol over the course of several days. Fermentation takes place faster at higher temperatures, and around 17 grams of sugar are needed to generate one degree of alcoholic strength.

If a winemaker wants to make a sweet wine, one way of doing this is to stop the fermentation early to leave residual sugar in the wine. Sometimes this will happen naturally: if the grapes are very rich in sugar, yeasts struggle to function as alcohol rises above 14 per cent. Other times, the winemaker will arrest the fermentation. Many German wines are made in this way, which explains their low levels of alcohol and high levels of sugar compared to other wines. If the winemaker is looking to make a dry wine, he or she will want to ferment all of the sugar out of the grapes.

The temperature of fermentation will significantly affect the character of a wine. As grape must ferments, the energy produced generates heat. Winemakers often control the temperature of the fermentation vessels to ensure consistent quality and to create the style of wine that they are aiming for. Cooler fermentation temperatures will bring the aromatics of the grapes to the fore, so grape varieties destined to be made into youthful, fragrant wines for early drinking will usually be fermented at cool temperatures. This would include aromatic grape varieties, such as Riesling, Sauvignon Blanc, Viognier and Muscat. A warmer fermentation will give a wine more structure and body, but less freshness of aroma. More age-worthy whites, which do not need to rely on primary, fruity aromas (Chardonnay, for example), are more likely to be fermented at slightly warmer temperatures.

For red wines, higher temperatures will extract more colour, tannins and flavour from the grapes. Reds fermented at cooler temperatures will have bright fruit character and more pronounced aromas, but less depth or structure. Although temperature control is now widely practised throughout the world, it is still more common in new world countries, partly for stylistic reasons and partly because the temperatures at harvest time tend to be warmer and so it is frequently necessary to cool the fermentation vats.

Try these

See if you can taste the difference in fermentation temperature in these wines:

- Cool-fermented whites: Australian Riesling, New Zealand Sauvignon Blanc
- Not-so-cool-fermented whites: Alsace Riesling (and other Alsace wines), other traditional French and Italian whites
- Cool-fermented red: Beaujolais Villages, France
- Warmer fermented red: Châteauneuf-du-Pape, France.

Red wine derives its colour from the skins, rather than from the flesh, of the grapes. To ensure that the wine is imbued with sufficient colour and tannin from the skins, various methods can be used to immerse the solid matter from the grapes in the liquid during the fermentation. Carbon dioxide is given off as a by-product of fermentation, and this gas rises through the fermenting must, carrying the skins, seeds and any other non-liquid matter to the top of the tank. This mass, known as the 'cap', must be immersed in the liquid in order for the wine to benefit from the colour, tannins and flavours in the skins.

When there is no more sugar to feed the yeasts, fermentation stops and carbon dioxide production ceases. The yeasts die and fall to the bottom of the tank, along with the rest of the grape matter. If more flavour and tannin extraction is desired, the wine is left to macerate with the skins for several days or weeks. The longer the wine is left with the residual grape matter, the higher the level of tannin in the wine will be and the more flavour will be drawn from the skins, but there is always a risk that excessive extraction can lead to bitterness and hard tannins, so long macerations are usually reserved for wines with a lot of structure, often destined for long bottle ageing. The heat given off during fermentation is useful in aiding extraction of the elements in the skins. Alcohol also increases extraction from the skins. The fermentation temperature and the extent of any post-fermentation maceration are key winemaking decisions that will influence the style of wine made.

Once the fermentation and maceration processes are complete, the wine is separated from the solid matter and put into storage vessels. The mass of solids and the small amount of liquid remaining is then pressed. The liquid produced is known as the press wine; it will taste harsh and bitter, but is particularly rich in matter from the grape skins. A winemaker may choose to add some or all of the press wine to the final wine to give extra body and structure.

Wild yeasts or commercial yeasts?

Most fermentations are not left to nature, but are started using commercial yeasts. This gives the winemaker greater control over the finished wine, since ambient yeasts may be less efficient or contain strains of wild yeast that will spoil the desired character of the wine. Some winemakers do prefer to let nature take its course though, particularly if the wine is made in smaller quantities. It is also far more common for premium wines. A widely held view is that using natural yeast develops more complex flavours in a wine, since there are different strains of yeast influencing the transformation of grapes to wine, rather than just one. In some cases, a wine is promoted as coming from a 'wild yeast ferment' on the label. For other wines, particular yeasts are chosen to bring out certain characters in the grapes, such as tropical flavours or floral notes.

Red, white or rosé?

The decision to make a red wine or a white wine is usually – with the notable exception of sparkling white wines made from Pinot Noir and Pinot Meunier – predetermined by the colour of the grapes. In theory, any colour of grape can be made into white wine, simply by pressing the grapes prior to fermentation, since the colour in red wines comes from the skins, not from the pulp. In practice, the value to be gained from macerating and fermenting black grapes with their skins is usually considered to be of greater value than not doing so, and few black grapes end up as white wine.

But what influences the decision to make rosé? There is probably no single answer to this, although commercial factors probably play as large a role as any other. One might think that grape varieties with naturally low colour might be better suited to make rosé wine, but there are many rosés made from grapes whose red wine equivalents are seldom short on colour: Cabernet Sauvignon, Syrah or Mourvèdre, for example. Producers with ambition to make 'serious' red wine will often make a rosé as a by-product of a red wine by 'bleeding' the red vat of some of its juice before or during fermentation. This will result in a more concentrated red wine and (as a bit of an afterthought) a rosé wine. Often the decision to make rosé seems to originate in local culture as much as in any innate quality of the wine. The warm, southern French region of Provence is a large producer of rosé wine. But is this because this is the wine best suited to the soil and climate of the area, or (perhaps more likely) because there is a ready market of tourists nearby on the Côte d'Azur, waiting to lap up the latest vintage each summer? Rosé is indisputably a perfect summer drink. It bridges the gap between red wine and white, having more structure and body than a white, but less weight and tannin than a red.

Try these

See if you can spot the similarity in flavour or structure between the following red, white and rosé wines, all made from the Pinot Noir grape:

- Blanc de noirs Champagne
- Sancerre rosé
- Red burgundy.

The art of blending

A wine is invariably defined by its place of origin. But in many instances winemakers will choose to blend grapes from different places – sometimes places that are very distant from each other – to make a particular, consistent style of wine. This is especially common in countries like Australia and the USA, where grapes from a large geographical area are blended together under a large regional appellation: for example, a wine labelled South Eastern Australia can come from four different states, an area that represents 98 per cent of the wine-growing land in Australia!

But a wine that is blended from different regions is not necessarily cheap, or of lesser quality. Australia's most famous wine, Grange, is a homage to the art of the winemaker. This is a multi-regional blend of grapes selected from fine vineyard sites across the country. Champagne, too, is a luxury wine made almost exclusively from blends: the wines are, in virtually every case, made up of grapes from vineyard sites across the large (and growing) Champagne appellation. Furthermore, all non-vintage (that is to say, non-dated) Champagnes, are a blend of wines from several years' crops. Here, the hand of the winemaker is key to defining the style of the wine.

Blending different vintages to create particular styles of wine is an art that has been perfected over generations by producers in other traditional regions of production as well. Tawny port with an age indication (10, 20 or 40 years) will be a blend of several vintages, giving an average age and taste that conforms to that expected on the label.

The solera system of sherry production practised in southern Spain involves a cascading system of barrels, whereby casks containing older wine are topped up with wine from the subsequent vintage. The older wines are refreshed with younger wine when a portion of the aged sherry is drawn from the barrels for bottling. Because the barrels are never fully emptied, any wine drawn from the oldest barrels will contain a percentage (however small) of the oldest wine of the solera, which is why some bottles of sherry indicate the age of the solera on the bottle. This system ensures that a consistency of style is produced, which limits vintage variation and ensures that the Fino or Amontillado in your glass will not taste substantially different from one year to the next. Each year, the youngest casks are topped up with wine from the new vintage.

To oak or not to oak?

The fashion for overtly oaky wines has waned. But this does not mean winemakers have stopped using oak. If you think you don't like oak, you should probably think again. Almost all great wine is made using oak in some fashion, and many other wines are also improved with oak. Oak can be used to subtle or bludgeoning effect in winemaking and is often a key determinant of a wine's style, even if you don't immediately notice this when you taste it.

Traditionally, wines were fermented in large oak casks and in some regions this is still often the case today. Some winemakers have reverted back to fermenting wine in oak in recent years, in the belief that advantages are derived from this natural material compared to the more modern, inert fermentation materials, such as stainless steel. Oak fermentation vessels are used not for the flavours of oak (which should be negligible in a large old cask), but for its physical properties. The small ingress of oxygen during fermentation in a wooden vat is thought to create a more harmonious wine from the outset, although it would take a very experienced taster indeed to spot this in a wine. Being thicker than stainless steel, oak also has the benefit of naturally maintaining a more stable temperature within the vat. The main disadvantage of fermenting in wood is that it requires scrupulous hygiene to ensure that bacteria do not get into the wood and taint the wine – a tainted wine is something most drinkers *would* notice.

Small oak barrels are commonly used for fermentation of high-quality white wines and for maturation of reds and whites. Small barrels, known as barriques (or *barricas*, in Spanish), typically hold the equivalent of 300 bottles of wine. They are only used for the best wines, as they are an expensive winemaking choice that will increase the price of the wine. White wines fermented in barrel will have less obvious oaky character than a wine that is put into barrel after fermentation. If you see a bottle with 'barrel fermented' on the label, you can expect a wine with some oak characteristics, but these should seem integrated and smooth, rather than woody or harsh.

A small barrel will have more impact on the flavour profile of a wine than a large one, due to the greater surface area of oak compared to wine. And a new barrel will have more effect on the flavour of a wine than an older one, because wine leaches flavours and tannins from the oak and these diminish over time. If you see that a wine has been aged in oak barriques (especially new ones), you can expect to find some significant oak-influenced character in the wine.

Oak is used more for maturation than for fermentation of red wines, and it is for maturation that its effects are the greatest. Here, the wine will evolve over an extended period of time – months or years, rather than the days spent fermenting – and the way it ages will depend to a great extent on the container it is in. In a stainless steel vat, sealed and blanketed by an inert gas such as carbon dioxide, for example, a wine will not change much, if at all. The only reason to keep a wine in such conditions is for storage before bottling. In a barrel, though, the slow exchange of air combines with the character of the wood to provide ideal conditions for ageing fine wines. Over a period of a year or more, the wine slowly achieves clarity and stability, the colour becomes deeper and the tannins become softer as a result of wood ageing.

Another decision for the winemaker is which type of oak to use. Of the many species of oak, few are suitable for use in wine production. Most common are French oak and American oak. American oak tends to give more powerful and sweeter flavours and a coarser texture of tannins compared to French oak, because the character of American oak is more quickly and easily absorbed into wine. American oak is often used for Australian Shiraz, red Rioja and other strongly flavoured wines from Spain and the new world. It is considerably cheaper than French oak, so it is a good option for mid-priced red wines to provide them with the benefits of oak maturation at a more economical price. French oak is highly prized because of its tight grain, which allows the wine to age slowly and acquire more refined, savoury, toasty aromas.

The flavours of oak come not just from the wood's provenance, but also from the way the barrel is made. Each barrel-maker will have a different style, and winemakers often use barrels from several producers to vary the flavours in their wines. The degree of 'toast' produced when making the barrel plays a large part in the presence of oak-derived flavours in the wine. A 'high-toast' barrel will impart strong, roasted, coffee, spicy aromas, whereas a 'medium-toast' barrel will have more toasty, cedary aromatics.

In short, there are many options for a winemaker to think about when it comes to oak. It's not uncommon for wineries to be permanently trialling different types of wood, different combinations of new and older oak, and different barrel-makers to try to get the balance of their wines exactly right.

There are several cheaper ways for a winemaker to get oak flavours into wine without buying expensive barrels. The most usual is to use oak chips, which are added to the grape must during fermentation. A wine labelled 'oaked' has probably been exposed to chips, or a similar alternative, oak staves, during its fermentation.

Identifying oak aromas and flavours

A surprising number of smells and tastes in wine come, at least in part, from oak. Here are some of the more common ones you might find:

- vanilla
- toast
- butter
- coconut
- tar
- ash
- mushroom
- sappy/green

- coffee
- nuts (hazelnuts, walnuts, almonds)
- cedar
- leather
- chocolate
- barbecue
- cinnamon
- clove
- woody/planky
- resin
- burnt
- smoke
- caramel
- toffee
- creamy
- tobacco
- bitter
- tannic.

How do different types of oak affect the taste of a wine?

Here's an oak experiment: try a comparison between three Chardonnay wines, one that is simply labelled 'oaked' (which will indicate that it was probably made with oak chips or staves), a second that is labelled 'barrel aged' (meaning it has been put into oak barrels or barriques after fermentation) and a third labelled 'barrel fermented'. Can you tell the difference? Notice how the wines feel in the mouth. Is the oak noticeable or harsh? Toasty or sweet? Do you find any of the nutty, spicy, smoky flavours noted above?

More winemaking tricks

Apart from the addition of flavour and texture from oak, there are many other ways winemakers can stamp their personal seal on a wine.

Malolactic fermentation

This is a term you only occasionally see referred to on a bottle, although its use is widespread. It is usually only mentioned as a point of difference for white wines, as red wines are routinely subjected to this process. The aims of malolactic fermentation are to reduce acidity and improve a wine's stability. It is a natural process that takes place after alcoholic fermentation, and is brought about by the action of lactic bacteria on the malic acid in the wine. It can occur naturally, as temperatures rise in springtime, but most winemakers prefer to inoculate their wine with bacteria to have greater control over the process. The tart, malic acid (such as is found in green apples) is converted into softer, lactic acid, with a by-product of carbon dioxide.

The effect on the wine is that it becomes less acidic, softer and more rounded. For reds it helps to stabilize colour and avoid vegetative aromas. For whites, the effects are more noticeable, because malolactic fermentation, as the name suggests, gives wines a certain lactic, creamy character. It also imparts a smoother texture. These characteristics can add interest to a more neutral grape, such as Chardonnay, but are less desirable for varieties that give crisp and fruity styles, such as Riesling. For a white wine with low acidity, a winemaker may decide to prevent malolactic fermentation taking place in order to preserve the freshness in the wine. Another option is to subject only a part of the wine to malolactic fermentation. When this is blended with the rest of the wine the result will be a wine with more complexity and a richer texture that is still sufficiently crisp to taste balanced.

Try these

To taste the effect of malolactic fermentation, try an oaky Chardonnay. The rich, buttery and lactic character tells you that the wine has undergone malolactic fermentation. If that's not a style you like, compare a wine made from Riesling or Sauvignon Blanc: it's very rare to find the flavours of malolactic fermentation in these wines.

Using the lees

This is another winemaking trick that can greatly affect style, especially the style of white wines. The lees are the sediment of dead yeast cells and grape matter that remain in the fermentation vessel after the fermentation has finished. Usually, the wine is decanted (racked) off the lees before its maturation to avoid any undesirable flavour exchanges taking place. But lees are very useful for some wines, as they can add richness and texture, along with certain yeasty flavours that complement some white varieties nicely (see also the section below on sparkling wines). Chardonnay is often enriched in this way. *Bâtonnage* is a word you may see on a label. It refers to the winemaking process of stirring up the lees on a regular basis in order to help the wine absorb more of their character and richness. It is a practice commonly used for high-quality, barrel-fermented whites, such as those from Bordeaux and Burgundy, but it may also play a part in more everyday white wines, such as Muscadet, where ageing on the lees (*'sur lie'*) is considered to improve the character of the wine sufficiently to warrant a separate mention in the appellation rules. This is an example of a rather neutral grape variety that is given some stuffing and yeasty interest by a period of tank ageing in contact with its lees.

Try these

To get a good idea of the effect of lees contact on a wine, try a Muscadet alongside a Muscadet sur lie. The latter should be richer, creamier, slightly yeasty and more full-bodied. Note that the lees effect on Muscadet will be less pronounced than for a wine that has undergone extended lees stirring and ageing in a barrel. Muscadet is probably the only wine that actually specifies within its appellation whether or not it has had any lees contact.

Adding bubbles

Any wine can be made to sparkle, but some styles of wine are far better suited to such treatment than others. Most sparkling wines are white or rosé, but there are a few successful reds, such as Australian sparkling Shiraz, or some traditional Italian and Portuguese reds. Other options available to the winemaker are to make the wine semi-sparkling, or to add a more subtle spritz for freshness. As with any decision, the winemaker should be looking to create a balanced product that best suits the raw material he or she has to work with.

Sparkling wine is defined as any wine that has carbon dioxide in it. At the most basic level, this could come from simple carbonation, which creates large bubbles that quickly disperse. More usual is a version of the traditional technique of promoting a second fermentation in a sealed bottle or tank. This results in a wine with an extra degree or so of alcohol, added flavour from the new fermentation and captured carbon dioxide. The quality of the bubbles and flavours in sparkling wine depends on three things: the quality of the base wine, the method of production, and the length of ageing.

Bubbles will accentuate any faults in a still wine, so the quality of the base wine is important, even if these wines are not very drinkable on their own, being generally low in flavour and very high in acidity. Grapes for sparkling wine are often picked earlier than other grapes, as a neutral and acidic base product is considered desirable. Strong grape flavours will compete with the characters looked for in sparkling wine, and a wine high in acidity will complement the carbon dioxide too and lift the wine. A sparkling wine low in acidity is liable to taste rather flat.

In the original and most famous sparkling wine region, Champagne, the most northerly vineyard area in France, the base wines are naturally light, crisp and fresh, with little flavour. More more neutral grape varieties are favoured for sparkling wine production (and often at very high yields, which further dilutes their flavour).

The original and best way to produce sparkling wine is by the method they use in Champagne. Because the Champenois are very protective of their name, you won't see the word Champagne on any bottles sold in Europe that don't actually come from the Champagne region. Instead, this method is called, variously, bottle-fermented, traditional method, *méthode traditionelle*, or sometimes, 'fermented in this bottle'.

The traditional method involves blending base wines together and then transferring the blend with a yeast and sugar mix into bottle (this is the same bottle the wine stays in until it is sold). The wines are then put into the cellar to ferment. The sugar gets to work straight away on the yeast, provoking a second fermentation in the bottle. The carbon dioxide produced from the fermentation is trapped in the sealed bottle and dissolves into the wine, creating the fizz. This takes place over a period of a few weeks.

More important than the fermentation is the ageing of the wine on the yeast lees that remain in the bottle once this second fermentation is complete. The best bottle-fermented wines are aged for long periods on their lees. Over this time they acquire distinctive flavours and aromas, by a process called yeast autolysis. The minimum period of ageing for wines in Europe is invariably defined by law, as this is such an important determinant of the wine's final style. For example, Cava and Crémant wines must be aged for a minimum of nine months on their lees. In Champagne, the requirements are far stricter. Non-vintage Champagne must spend at least 15 months ageing in the cellars, and for vintage Champagne the minimum period is three years. This is the reason that the average vintage Champagne will always show more of this leesy, autolytic character than a non-vintage Champagne. If you get the chance, try one of each style from the same producer to see the difference.

Once the wines have been aged on the lees, all that remains is to remove the lees from the wine. This is done by a process known as riddling. The bottles, lying on their sides in the cellar, are turned sharply to the side once a day over a period of weeks. At the same time, the bottle is inclined slightly more each day so that the accumulated sediment of lees moves gradually towards the neck of the bottle. Traditionally done by hand, this is now largely an automated process and achieved over a much shorter period. With the sediment collected in the neck of the now upside-down bottle, the winemaker immerses the top of the neck in a solution of brine to freeze the captured sediment. With the sediment safely frozen, the bottle can be turned the right way up and opened. The pressure inside the bottle from the carbon dioxide gas will cause the pellet of ice containing the sediment to shoot out of the bottle, taking with it a little wine. This is replaced by the *liqueur de dosage*, made from older wine and a little sugar, depending on the sweetness required in the wine. Even a wine labelled *Brut* will have a little sugar to balance the crispness of the wine. A few wines are made with no *dosage* at all.

A variation on the traditional method is the tank method. As the name suggests, the second fermentation takes place in a sealed tank. This less labour-intensive method is used for cheaper sparkling wines, such as Prosecco, and these wines will not show the autolytic character from lees ageing that can be found in bottle-fermented wines.

To give a wine a little sparkle, or to preserve freshness in a wine that may have low levels of acidity, some producers will add a little carbon dioxide to a wine at the time of bottling. This will be noticeable as a little spritz on the palate and is usually quite a pleasant addition to a wine. Many Italian whites have this character.

Filtration

This is a common practice for most wines. It is done to remove solid matter from wine and to ensure its microbial stability. However, you may come across wine labels that tell you the wine has not been filtered (it may also say the wine has not been fined, another winemaking process that serves to clarify and stabilize wine). Fining and filtration are sometimes eschewed on the grounds that these processes are harmful to fine wine, especially when done to the fine degree that renders wine sterile. If a wine is made and bottled quickly, it is more likely that it will need to be stabilized by filtration than if it has already spent time ageing slowly in a small barrel, a process that encourages natural stabilization.

Fortification

This is another option available to winemakers. This means adding spirit, which will increase the wine's alcoholic strength. The alcohol in the spirit will stop any fermentation, so for sweet wines, such as port, the spirit will be added during fermentation, whereas for fortified wines that are essentially dry, such as sherry, it will be added afterwards.

Bottling options

Arguably, the stopper used to close a wine should not affect the way it tastes, but in the wine industry this is a subject of intense debate. Have you noticed just how much of the wine from New Zealand is sealed with a screwcap? Take a look. The switch away from cork has been remarkable here and is a trend that is also taking hold in many other parts of the world.

The reason for the shift is due to producers' dissatisfaction with natural cork, due to its imperfect seal (which can cause a wine to oxidize prematurely) and to the occasional presence of the chemical trichloroanisole (or TCA), which is responsible for the musty taint referred to as 'cork taint'. Wine that is 'corked' is tainted with TCA. TCA destroys wine quality. Even if you don't notice that a wine tainted with TCA is faulty, it's unlikely you'll enjoy it. TCA is a problem that the cork industry has been unable to eradicate, and which has led to alternative closures being trialled and now adopted on a large scale by winemakers.

While natural cork is still the most widespread choice for sealing a bottle, producers are turning to plastic, glass and screwcaps as alternatives. The challenge is to find a stopper that is inert, so will not influence the flavour profile of the wine, and one that will provide an effective seal. The greatest excitement surrounds the use of screwcaps. It used to be that only the cheapest wines were sealed this way, but this is no longer the case. Although many remain unconvinced of the ability of red wines to age under screwcaps (perhaps because there is insufficient history yet to prove it), the case for the suitability of screwcaps to seal white wines, and especially aromatic white wines, is strong. Wines sealed in this way retain all of their vibrant fruit and aromatics, which probably explains New Zealanders' keenness to embrace a product that highlights the natural qualities of their wines.

06

understanding your own taste

In this chapter you will learn:
- why the way you taste is unique to you
- how to tell if you are a 'supertaster'
- how your senses can fool you.

If you've ever been at a loss to understand the appeal of a wine that other people tell you is great, don't worry. It's not that you have no taste – more than likely, it's simply that your sense of taste is different from theirs. The growing body of research into how we experience taste and smell suggests that our sensory appreciation of wine may be as unique as our fingerprints.

Objective and subjective measures of a wine

There is a difference between the objective way a wine can be measured and the subjective way you experience it. Any wine can be analyzed to show its composition in terms of alcohol content, acidity levels, residual sugar, and even the quantity and type of tannins that are present. So, we can say with certainty that a wine with 15 per cent alcohol is high in alcohol, since we know that most wines are closer to 13 per cent. In the same way, we can measure the tannins in a young red wine from Bordeaux and even see that there are fewer present in an older vintage of the same wine, where some of the tannins have fallen as deposit into the bottom of the bottle.

Most people, with a degree of practice, can learn to distinguish these known facts about wine. As explained earlier, the structural elements of wine are a key part of learning how to distinguish one wine from another. But your subjective reaction to the wine – how much you actually like it – is another matter altogether.

Much of wine education is termed wine 'appreciation'. This term implies that you are unable to appreciate wine unless you learn something about it first. This is not the case. It is true that you can learn from a book, or a class, or from reading a wine critic's scores, which wines are widely accepted by others as being good or less good. And by learning about wine you will have the opportunity to taste wines you have not tasted before (hopefully this is now the case, if you have been tasting your way through this book). By doing this, you will certainly make some new discoveries that you like. Another likelihood is that the more you taste high-quality wine, the harder it will be to go back to wines with a less interesting array of flavours, textures and aromas. You can learn to appreciate wine more merely by exposing yourself to its variety and complexity. But, in spite of all this, even if you have all the wine education in the world, what is unlikely to change is your own, singular perception of the objectively measurable elements of wine. In other words, your personal taste is unlikely to change very much.

Why your palate is unique

None of us has the same face or the same fingerprints – or the same palate. Just as you prefer one food to another, so your preferences in wine will differ from the next person's. It sounds obvious, but when it comes to wine, common sense often seems to fly out of the window. I have many times heard people who think they don't know about wine say they would be not be able to appreciate a good wine. Novice wine drinkers seem to feel that their ignorance is somehow a barrier to enjoyment, or the reason for their not liking a particular wine. They would probably have no such insecurities about claiming to like or dislike a new type of vegetable, brand of chocolate, or pair of shoes.

The reasons for your individual preferences are twofold. The first factor to consider is your physiology; the second, your personal experience. Both will influence your senses of taste and smell.

The physical nature of taste

As we have seen in Chapter 02, our tongues are of relatively limited use when trying to ascertain the taste of a wine. Compared to our noses, which can identify tens of thousands of smells and nuances of quality, our palates can manage a mere five flavours: sweet, sour, salty, bitter and savoury (or umami – see Chapter 10 for more about this). Nevertheless, these five tastes play a large part in determining whether or not we like a wine and whether we find it to be in balance. The sensitivity of our palates is thought to depend principally on the number of taste buds we have, and this varies from person to person.

American experimental psychologist, Dr Linda Bartoshuk, coined the term 'supertaster' to describe the estimated 25 per cent of the population who taste more intensely than the majority. If you are female, or of Asian or African ethnicity, you are more likely to fall into this group. Around 50 per cent of us have 'normal' sensitivities and the remaining 25 per cent of 'non-tasters' have less sensitive palates than the average.

This discovery has significant implications for understanding which wines and foods you will enjoy. A supersensitive palate will be less tolerant of bitterness, alcohol and strong flavours in general. Contrary to what the term might suggest, supertasters may struggle to enjoy wine at all. And if they do, they are more likely to choose delicately flavoured wines that are lower in alcohol and perhaps slightly sweet. Non-tasters, on the other hand, are less sensitive to alcohol, often reporting it to be sweet in flavour rather than burning. For these tasters, bigger is usually better. They will tend to prefer beefy red wines with strong flavours. For them, bitterness from tannins is not a problem. It is thought that many of the most influential male wine critics fall into this category.

Are you a supertaster?

The easiest way to get an idea of your own palate's relative sensitivity is to examine the tip of your tongue in a mirror. What you are looking for are the raised bumps called 'fungiform papillae' that house your taste buds. They are easier to see if you dab a little food colouring on your tongue, as the papillae do not absorb the colour. A dense concentration of small fungiform papillae indicates that you have heightened taste sensitivity. As a guide, place the hole from a hole-punched piece of paper over the tip of your tongue. The average person will have some 15 visible fungiform papillae within this area. For a supertaster, the figure will be double or more. Non-tasters will have fewer, larger taste buds that are more spread out.

Another way of determining your sensitivity is to think about the kinds of foods you like and dislike. Non-tasters tend to like most food, regardless of its preparation, whereas supertasters are more fussy (although there are obviously many other reasons for food preferences that may override biological ones). Supertasters are likely to avoid strong black coffee, grapefruit and bitter-tasting leafy vegetables such as broccoli and brussels sprouts. They are also more likely to add salt to their food to compensate for the bitterness they find hard to tolerate.

Why we don't all smell in the same way

We have 350 different receptor genes for smell. Researchers have found that 75 of these genes vary across individuals. Some will be intact, some intact but mutated, and some will be non-functional. We tend to assume that we all smell things fairly equally, but there are great differences in the way we perceive even quite common smells. For example, there is a billion-fold difference in individuals' sensitivity to musk. According to Dr Charles Wysocki, of the Monell Chemical Senses Center in Philadelphia, 43 per cent of us can't smell it at all. The phenomenon of being unable to smell something readily detected by others (known as specific anosmia) is more common than you might think. Wysocki reckons that everyone has at least one (and probably more) of these smell disabilities.

Things you may not be able to smell:

- Amyl acetate – bananas, pears
- Bagdanol analog – sandalwood
- Benzyl salycilate – balsamic, sweet, floral
- Galaxolide – musky
- Androstenone – urinous, woody, floral.

Our own sensory worlds

Quite apart from our physical differences, our perception of smells will vary depending on our culture and life experience. Our olfactory sense is the sense most closely linked to our emotions and our memory. A scant breath of a scent can evoke powerful feelings in an instant. Yeasty smells, bread aromas, floral scents, fresh hay, lanolin, leather ... and hundreds of other aromas, can create an emotional response. Our emotional reaction to the aromas of a wine will naturally play a part in how much we like it. In research conducted by Dr Alan Hirsch, a specialist in human olfaction based in Chicago, 86 per cent of individuals tested had vivid memory associations with certain aromas. These associations are usually positive, but can be negative. For example, Hirsch found that the smell of cut grass produced more positive feelings in those born before 1960, but less positive feelings amongst younger adults, for whom the smell of cut grass carried an association of being forced to mow the grass as a child. How you respond to smells will vary according to your genetic make-up and cultural and environmental influences as well. When it comes to smell and taste, we are all, to a large extent, in our own sensory worlds. We each have our own perception of reality.

Your senses might be fooling you

Wines bought on holiday just never taste quite as good when you get them home; why is that? Did the wine match the local cuisine especially well? Or did it not travel well? Perhaps it's more likely that you are the one who didn't travel so well. The importance of context, expectations – even our mood – in affecting our sensory experiences should not be underestimated.

Did you know?

Even the professionals can be duped. Here's a confession from a UK supermarket buyer: 'The first commercial wine purchase I ever made was a Catalan white. I went over and the bloke took me out for lunch. We had paella overlooking the sea in Barcelona and I ordered 500 cases. The wine came in November and when we sat down in the tasting room, my boss looked at me and we both agreed it was vinegar.'

Our brains can fool us very easily. For example, your sense of smell functions to detect new odours. But your brain will quickly adapt to smells that are already there, even quite strong ones, and tune them out of your consciousness, just so long as they don't change. Each new smell or change in smell will send your smell receptors back to work. That's the reason why the smell of cooking that is so appetizing when you walk into a room rapidly appears to dissipate: your brain just adapts to it and switches the smell off. Some professional tasters try to refresh their olfactory sense by sniffing coffee or bread between wines.

Our expectations can alter our appreciation of flavours and aromas. At a seminar I attended a couple of years ago, delegates were each given a tube containing a pungent, cheesy aroma. Half of the tubes were labelled 'food' and the other half 'body'. The people who had been given the suggestion of food were far more appreciative of the smell than the 'body' group, who associated the aroma with bodily odours and smelly socks.

A simpler example is to consider how easy it is to be fooled by the mere colour of a wine. There are numerous instances of tasters being fooled into writing tasting notes describing a red wine for a white wine coloured red. Try tasting wine completely blind and see if you can even tell if it is red or white. You might be surprised at how difficult it is!

Can music affect the way wine tastes?

It sounds far-fetched, but researchers at Scotland's Herriot Watt University have come up with research that suggests playing different types of music can influence our perceptions of the taste of a wine. While they were given a glass of wine to drink, the participants in the study could hear a piece of background music of one of four styles ('powerful and heavy', 'mellow and soft', 'subtle and refined', or 'zingy and refreshing'). They were then asked to rate the wine and its characteristics compared to these descriptors. The researchers found a significant correlation between the type of music that people were listening to and their interpretation of the style of the wine.

In another study, researchers showed that playing accordion music in a supermarket increased sales of French wine over German wine by five bottles to one. Conversely, playing oompah music increased sales of German wine over French by two to one. So, the next time you're buying wine, check what type of music they are playing in the shop.

part three

wines of the world

07

how to identify wine styles

In this chapter you will learn:
- what components of wine influence its style
- how to make comparisons between different wine styles through tasting
- how to use knowledge of wine styles to select wine for different occasions
- how to identify the style of wine that's right for you.

Now that you have had the chance to practise tasting and to experience the differences between grape varieties, you'll already have developed your preferences. The next step is to refine these preferences further by looking at wine styles. This will enable you to identify similar wines to those you know you like, and highlight why you like them.

It will also be helpful when choosing wine in a shop or restaurant, or when choosing wine for others. And in a restaurant, if you are able to communicate the style of wine you like to the waiter, you are far more likely to end up with a wine you like, even if you don't recognize anything on the wine list.

This chapter describes the main styles of red and white wine, giving examples and suggestions for tasting comparisons to do at home. There are many different ways of classifying wine. The more you taste, the more you will develop your own sense of the style, or styles, of wines that you like. Here, you will notice that some wines appear in more than one category. This is because the same wine can come in different styles; for example, there are different styles of Pinot Gris from Alsace. Information about the style of a wine is often given on the back label of the bottle, so this will help if you are buying in a shop. If you are in a restaurant, don't be shy about asking about the style of wine you are buying.

Key white wine styles

- light and fizzy (page 101)
- aromatic, fruity and dry (page 103)
- light and neutral (page 105)
- mineral and food-friendly (page 106)
- creamy and rich (page 108)
- medium-dry to medium-sweet (page 110)
- sweet and luscious (page 112).

The pages that follow will lead you through sample tastings of wines that fit these styles. If you can, try to taste them all to get a greater understanding of which wines to choose to suit your needs. To help you decide which styles you are likely to prefer without tasting everything there is to taste, it helps to ask yourself a few questions.

Do you prefer ...	Try these styles
strong flavours?	aromatic, fruity and dry; sweet and luscious
more neutral flavours?	light and neutral; light and fizzy
the taste of oak?	creamy and rich
powerful aromas?	aromatic, fruity and dry; sweet and luscious
wines with texture?	mineral and food-friendly; creamy and rich; sweet and luscious
wine to drink right away?	most wines, especially aromatic, fruity and dry; light and neutral; light and fizzy
something you can keep?	mineral and food-friendly; sweet and luscious; creamy and rich
full-bodied wine?	creamy and rich; sweet and luscious
light-bodied wine?	light and fizzy; light and neutral
something not too dry?	medium-dry to medium-sweet; creamy and rich; sweet and luscious
wine to drink with food?	light and neutral; mineral and food-friendly
wine to drink without food?	light and fizzy; aromatic, fruity and dry; medium-dry to medium-sweet; sweet and luscious

Light and fizzy

This style covers a wide range of prices, sweetness levels and drinking occasions. What the wines all share is their fresh fizz. There is something about bubbles in wine that is automatically festive, and it doesn't cost much to get a party going with inexpensive sparkling wine. For any kind of big celebration, Champagne is a natural choice, but there are some very good sparkling wines that rival Champagne for quality and price from England, Australia (especially Tasmania), New Zealand and the USA. Sweeter sparkling styles are lovely for the end of a meal, or for outdoor summer drinking.

Try these

- Moscato d'Asti from Italy
- Cava from Spain
- Champagne from France
- Australian sparkling wine labelled 'traditional method'.

Sparkling wine should never feel heavy and should always taste fresh. Compared to other wines, the flavours of sparkling wines are usually less pronounced.

At the lighter end of this style are the sweeter wines, such as Moscato d'Asti and other semi-sparkling Italian wines, labelled *frizzante*. When an aromatic grape variety is used, the wines are more likely to take on the character of the grape; when made with a more neutral base wine, the style of the wine will be determined more by the ageing process than the grape variety. A prolonged ageing of more than 18 months will result in a wine with a style that is more yeasty, bready, appley, brioche-like or toasty. These are the wines that cost more and taste like Champagne.

Aromas, flavours and structure

When you pour the wines, look at the stream of bubbles. A fine, persistent stream of tiny bubbles is an indication of quality in sparkling wine. When you taste the wine, notice how the mousse feels. Are the bubbles sharp and unpleasant, or small, soft and mousse-like? How persistent are the flavours? Sparkling wine can be hard to taste because of all the bubbles. To make it easier, leave the wine in your glass for 15 minutes and then come back to it. Notice how it has changed. Has the fizz gone? Does it taste better or worse? A good quality sparkling wine should still taste good.

Asti is a fragrant and undemanding wine, sweetly grapey and low in alcohol. It is a light and summery drink that can be enjoyed on its own, with a light dessert, or even instead of a dessert.

Cava is made from local Spanish grape varieties (Xarel-lo, Parellada and Macabeo – plus, sometimes, Chardonnay). You'll find a clean and crisp, dry wine, with quite neutral, slightly earthy aromas and flavours. It's an inexpensive, festive drink that can be enjoyed any time you fancy some bubbles.

Champagne styles vary, but you should notice that this wine has more of a yeasty, biscuity character compared to the first two wines. This is due to the extended period of ageing (for more about this see Chapter 05). Few sparkling wines from other parts of the world are aged for this long prior to release. For new world wines you can often find this information on the back label of the bottle.

The Australian wine will probably have more pronounced aromas, and possibly a deeper colour, compared to the other wines. This is due to the warmer, sunnier climate from which it hails compared to the European wines. Australian sparkling wine typically follows the Champagne use of grape varieties of Pinot Noir, Chardonnay and Pinot Meunier, so its aromas and flavours will be similar.

Look out for light and fizzy wines from:

- France: Crémant wines from many areas; Blanquette de Limoux; Saumur Brut
- Italy: Prosecco
- Portugal: Vinho Verde
- New Zealand
- USA: Napa; Anderson Valley
- England.

Aromatic, fruity and dry

Perhaps the easiest group of wines to enjoy are highly perfumed, light white wines that derive their aromas from fresh, ripe fruit. What defines the wines in this category is the allure of their youthful scent, which is frequently accompanied by refreshing acidity. These wines may occasionally be aged in oak, but this is not a perceptible part of their style. Aromatic whites may be delicate or pungent. They are usually made from a single grape variety with a strong individual character.

These wines are suited to drinking alone to enjoy their pure, fresh flavours, or with food. They are medium-bodied with moderate alcohol. Their bright, powerful flavours are often successful with spicy foods.

Try these

- Dry Muscat from Alsace, France
- Gewurztraminer from Alto Adige, Italy
- Sauvignon Blanc from South Africa
- Riesling from Clare Valley, Australia.

For preference, choose a recent vintage.

Aromas, flavours and structure

You may notice a few bubbles of carbon dioxide when you pour these wines – added to keep the wines fresh. Think about the range of different scents these wines present and try to distinguish between them. Each wine should smell quite distinct. Do they smell sweet or dry? These are wines that often smell sweet, but taste dry.

The Muscat is likely to smell of grapes and flowers (roses, honeysuckle). If you've done the previous tasting, see how your note compares with the Moscato from Italy. It is delicate and 'pretty', and intensely perfumed. Muscat from Alsace smells sweet, but is dry. It is probably also lighter in weight than its strong aromas suggest.

Gewurztraminer smells of roses and lychees and spice. Some people find its perfume overwhelming, but the variety typically has a lighter and more restrained florality when it is grown in northern Italy. The wine will almost certainly be dry, but will probably smell sweet. It may even taste a little sweet, even if it is not. This is because Gewurztraminer is a wine with very low levels of natural acidity. Without the lift of acidity on the finish, Gewurztraminer's pungent, floral character can fool you into thinking it is sweet.

The Sauvignon Blanc will have grassy, nettly, pungent, mainly green aromas (rather than aromas of fruits), but it can also have floral scents (especially elderflower). This is a predictable wine: it delivers on the palate exactly what it promises on the nose, every time – a crisp, green, mouth-watering freshness in the mouth. Perhaps this is what makes new world Sauvignon Blanc such a popular choice: it is the no-surprises grape, with a guaranteed, recognizable character and full fruitiness on the palate.

The Riesling will have mouth-watering aromas, often reminiscent of citrus fruits (especially lime) and white flowers. Older examples may have mineral or diesel/petrol scents. This probably tastes the crispest of this group of four wines. The citrus quality of the flavours should reflect the aromas. This wine may seem more challenging to drink than the soft and easy flavours of Muscat and Gewurztraminer, or the bright and simple Sauvignon. Riesling's acidity gives it an austerity that is often not appreciated, especially by newcomers to wine.

Look out for aromatic, fruity and dry whites from:

- France: Alsace (Gewurztraminer); Languedoc (Sauvignon Blanc, Viognier); Bordeaux (Sauvignon Blanc)
- Spain: Rueda; Rias Baixas (Albariño)
- Chile: Gewurzrtraminer, Sauvignon Blanc
- Germany: Riesling
- Austria: Riesling
- New Zealand: Sauvignon Blanc, Riesling
- England: Bacchus
- Argentina: Salta (Torrontès)
- USA: unoaked Sauvignon Blanc
- Australia: wines from Verdelho and Sauvignon Blanc.

Light and neutral

These are the types of wines that slip down almost unnoticed. They could be seen as the opposite style from the aromatic, fruity wines, although they do provide crisp, dry drinking in the same way. They are more likely to be from Europe, as they are not characterized by ripe, forward fruit. They are also likely to be cheaper wines, as they are often produced from high-yielding vines that give grapes with limited flavour concentration. These wines are safe, if unexciting, choices for a group, with or without food.

Try this selection to see if your preferences are more towards the neutral. If you like these, you'll probably also enjoy the following section of mineral and food-friendly wines, which are in a similar style, but with more wide-ranging flavours.

Try these
- Pinot Grigio from Italy
- Muscadet from France
- Viura (or Rioja) from Spain.

Aromas, flavours and structure

These are not, on the whole, wines looking to be noticed. Aromas and flavours are not pronounced. At best, these wines should be light and well balanced, and offer crisp, easy refreshment above all. Alcohol will probably be moderate to low for all of these wines, making them good with food or as a light aperitif, or inexpensive party wine. With food, their mild flavours will be unobtrusive.

When you taste these wines, notice how they compare to the strong flavours of the aromatic wines above, or to the light, fresh, sparkling wines. What are the obvious features of these wines? Is this style of wine what you feel most comfortable drinking? How do the wines feel in your mouth? Soft? Fresh? Savoury? Delicate?

The Pinot Grigio will have light, nutty, slightly oily characters and feel soft in the mouth, possibly with a touch of sweetness. Acidity will be quite low compared to most of the aromatic and sparkling wines.

The Muscadet will have little obvious fruitiness, but may well taste quite yeasty in character. It will probably taste a little crisper than the Pinot Grigio, but have a similarly soft feel to it.

The Viura will be lightly floral in its aromas, unless it has been made with some oak, in which case these aromas will dominate. It is medium-bodied with quite low acidity, making it feel gentle on the palate.

Look out for light and neutral whites from:

- France: Burgundy (Aligoté); Bordeaux (Entre-Deux-Mers); Loire Valley (Anjou)
- Italy: north and centre (e.g. Frascati, Trebbiano, Soave)
- Australia: Colombard
- South Africa: cheaper Chenin Blanc.

Mineral and food-friendly

These wines are less showy and have less immediate, fruity appeal than the perfumed, aromatic varieties, but they are flexible wines that are likely to please many people if you need to choose wine for a group. If you like your wine to taste less obviously of fruits and vegetables, you may find you prefer these more understated examples, all of which are dry.

Since the grapes used to make these wines have less natural aromatic potential, winemaking techniques that bring out other aromas, such as oak, or other qualities, such as texture, are often used. These wines often undergo some kind of oak ageing or lees ageing (for more on these techniques, see Chapter 05).

Try these
- Chablis from France
- Grüner Veltliner from Austria
- Fino sherry from Spain
- Savennières from the Loire Valley, France.

Wines most readily available will be recent vintages, although these wines can often age well (with the exception of Fino sherry), since they do not rely for their appeal on fresh, vibrant fruitiness.

Aromas, flavours and structure

You will notice that these wines are less effusive compared to the aromatic, fruity style, although their aromas are no less enticing, once you know what to look for. These wines will all be dry, medium in weight, with a range of predominantly non-fruit flavours. Their flavours should not differ greatly from the aromas. When you taste these wines focus on the intensity of the flavours and their savoury minerality. You may find that you want to sip these wines more slowly than lighter, fruitier styles. The main expected comparisons here are in the weight and texture of the fruit.

Chablis has muted but distinct aromas that are nothing really to do with fruit and everything to do with the place the grapes are grown. The scent is mineral, stony, salty and savoury, and sometimes lifted with a touch of creamy oak. The dryness of this wine gives it a firm, steely texture that makes it rather hard to drink on its own, but very good with food. More expensive examples (labelled Premier Cru and Grand Cru) will show greater concentration of the unique Chablis character.

Grüner Veltliner has a lightly lemony aroma, but is more nutty than fruity, with yeasty, almond notes. This is probably the most obviously fruity wine of this group (you will find all wines from Austria are pleasantly fruity). You may notice that the acidity, although high in this wine, seems less austere than the Chablis, due to its slightly more generous fruit.

Fino sherry carries unmistakable, sharp aromas and flavours of the flor yeast under which the wine matures in cask. It is deeply savoury, unusually tangy, salty and mineral, but without the refreshing acidity of the previous two wines. This is a powerfully flavoured wine with no trace of fruitiness. Try it with different foods, rather than just as a pre-dinner drink. Its taste matches many foods very well. This wine is also medium-bodied, although its alcohol is high (over 15 per cent).

Savennières, made from the Chenin Blanc grape, has an individual, highly mineral aroma that includes wax and honey and possibly baked apple, but never hints at fresh fruit. It might also smell slightly bitter. It is medium to full in weight. Its palate may taste quite honeyed initially, but it finishes dry, often leaving a lick of bitterness in the mouth.

Look out for mineral and food-friendly whites from:

- France: Burgundy; Alsace; Bordeaux
- Italy: most good quality Italian whites fit this category
- Spain: Rioja
- Portugal
- Greece: many good, savoury wines, especially from Assyrtiko grapes
- South Africa: from Chardonnay or Chenin Blanc
- New Zealand: from Chardonnay
- Australia: made from Sémillon
- Hungary: dry styles made from Furmint.

Creamy and rich

These are hedonistic wines, concentrated and full-bodied, though still essentially dry. Their appeal lies more in their texture and depth of flavour than simple, fruity refreshment. There are wines available at different quality levels in this style. At the most basic level, they include inexpensive, oaky Chardonnays from the new world. Further up the scale are some of the most alluring and satisfying white wines you can find. They can be very versatile with food and, as they have no hardness or sharp edges, they are also good to drink alone. Be aware that the alcohol levels of these wines may be higher than for other styles. Use of oak and other winemaking treatments can create rich, round and creamy characters, but not all wines in this style will be oaky. If you like your wine to taste full and ripe, this is a style for you.

Try these

- Meursault from Burgundy, France
- Condrieu from the Rhône Valley, France
- Pinot Gris from New Zealand
- Chardonnay from Napa Valley, California, USA.

Aromas, flavours and structure

These wines tend to be higher in alcohol than lighter weight and fruitier styles. This will be noticeable if you swirl the glass and observe how the wine clings to the sides. You will smell oak on a few of these wines.

In the Meursault, you can expect to find rich, nutty flavours allied with toasty oak and a smooth, but crisp palate. Although full-bodied for Burgundy, this is likely to be the least rich of these four wines.

Unless the Napa Chardonnay specifies that it is unoaked, it will have toasty, creamy, vanilla aromas from the wine's contact with oak. The Meursault will also have an oak influence, more in the savoury, toasty vein than sweet vanilla. Condrieu is a beautifully aromatic wine, with scents of apricots and peaches, and possibly some creamy oak notes as well. Pinot Gris is not usually a very aromatic variety, but the full-flavoured New Zealand style typically throws up a tropical cocktail of aromas, from pineapple to mango and lychee.

Condrieu is made from the fragrant and naturally low-acid Viognier grape. Viognier wines are rarely exciting in other parts of the world, but in the northern Rhône Valley this grape variety produces gloriously rich wines with flavours as intense as their aromas. Freshness is replaced by concentration. Notice the length of flavour in this wine – a sign of quality.

New Zealand Pinot Gris is in a similar style to Condrieu, but with more obvious fruitiness and usually more noticeable alcohol. Its texture often seems quite oily.

California Chardonnay is known for its ripe, creamy, buttery flavours, and although recent styles are moving away from the super-ripe, this is still the place to find big wines with an oak polish. Alcohol is usually quite high – perhaps as high as 15 per cent.

Look out for creamy and rich whites from:

- France: northern Rhône (from Crozes-Hermitage, Hermitage, St Joseph); Alsace (especially Gewurztraminer and Pinot Gris and dry, late-harvest wines); other riper Burgundy styles (such as Pouilly-Fuissé and Grand Cru Chablis)
- USA: most whites fit the riper and richer style, especially oaked Chardonnnay
- Australia: Chardonnay, Marsanne.

Medium-dry to medium-sweet

This is the broadest group here, as it is defined principally by sweetness. It is included as a separate category purely because sweetness can be such a dominant element of wine that it is good to identify where sweetness is found. This is often easier said than done: of all the styles of wine, those that are off-dry are hardest to identify by the label alone. The wines here include fresh and fruity Rieslings and food-friendly Chenin Blancs.

Try these

- Vouvray from the Loire Valley, France
- inexpensive Chardonnay from California, USA
- Pinot Gris from Alsace, France
- Riesling Spätlese from Germany.

When buying these wines, look out for 'Demi-Sec' on the Vouvray and 'Vendanges Tardives' (meaning 'late harvest') on the Pinot Gris. For the Riesling Spätlese (this word also means late harvest), avoid any bottle mentioning the word 'trocken'. This means 'dry', although a wine labelled this way may still have some sweetness. (Yes, it's highly confusing for all of us!)

Aromas, flavours and structure

Tasting sweeter wines may seem easy, but it can be difficult. The key thing to try to do is to look beyond the sweetness, which may be the main thing you notice in your mouth. Sugar is a large determinant of this style, but it is the balancing effect of the other components in each wine that will help you to establish its overall quality, whether you feel like a second glass and how well the wine might age. A talented winemaker will achieve the right balance between ripe fruit, alcohol and acidity.

When you hold these wines in your mouth, look for acidity that will freshen the feel of the wine. The presence or absence of acidity is the main factor determining whether you can taste the amount of sweetness in a wine. In the lightweight German Spätlese Riesling wine it should be easy to identify the sugar and the acidity, as both are high. Notice the effect this combination has on the wine. It will taste sweet as it enters the mouth, but the acidity quickly counters the sweetness.

Vouvray is made from the Chenin Blanc grape and often smells of straw, honey and wet wool. Poorer examples can be a little musty. This demi-sec wine will seem quite weighty in the mouth, but the high-acid Chenin grapes from which it is made will lift the wine, giving it a refreshingly crisp finish, even if it is quite sweet.

The California wine will smell rich and creamy and perhaps buttery. You may smell sweet vanilla or toasty aromas from oak here. If your Californian Chardonnay has been exposed to some kind of oak during the winemaking process, this may be the most noticeable thing about the wine. It may have a toasty, vanilla character, and you may even notice some textural effect of the oak tannins drying your mouth and teeth. This is not a wine that will ever be labelled 'sweet', and it may in fact be completely dry. Even if there is no residual sugar, the ripeness of the fruit imparts sweet flavours of melon, peach, and mango that, if not offset by acidity, make the wine appear off-dry. The effects of malolactic fermentation (see Chapter 05), a technique commonly used to enrich Chardonnay, reinforce this impression, giving the wine buttery flavours and a smooth mouth-feel.

The Pinot Gris from Alsace will be fruitier in style, in the soft and possibly tropical spectrum. Expect bananas and peachy fruit here. It has a similar type of profile in the mouth to a new world Chardonnnay, with ripe, easy, tropical fruit flavours, full body and relatively low acidity. Picked late, it can easily achieve high levels of alcohol when fermented, so choosing to leave some of the excess sugar unfermented in the wine helps to keep the wine balanced. Even Pinot Gris with no residual sugar can taste off-dry, due to the rich weight of fruit in the mouth.

The Riesling should be the most aromatic of this group of four; Riesling is typically mouthwateringly fresh and alive. The aromas of Riesling depend on where it is grown, but in Germany young Riesling is characterized by aromas of white flowers and crisp fruits such as apples, lemons and grapefruit. A wine like this could easily have 40 grams per litre of residual sugar, yet taste no sweeter than a Pinot Gris with 10 grams of sugar per litre, because Riesling always has firm, high acid levels compared to Pinot Gris. A wine with high acidity will taste less sweet than a wine with low acidity.

Look out for medium-dry to medium-sweet whites from:

- France: other Alsace wines, especially from Gewurztraminer. Some producers make more off-dry wines than others; Loire (Coteaux du Layon)
- Italy: Pinot Grigio; Moscato d'Asti
- USA: most large brands of white wine; pink (labelled 'white') Zinfandel
- Portugal: less sweet Madeiras – Sercial and Verdelho.

Sweet and luscious

Sweet wine has rather fallen from fashion with today's preference for drier or medium styles. These wines are worth seeking out and are a real treat to drink at the end of a meal. You may find they seem expensive, but due to their richness you probably won't want to drink too much. They are usually sold in smaller bottles. These are wines that can be tough to match with food. If you plan to serve sweet wine with dessert, make sure the wine is at least as sweet as the dessert, or the sweetness of the food will diminish your enjoyment of the wine. Best of all, drink sweet wines on their own. These are some of the most delicious drinks in the world.

Try these

- Sauternes from France
- Tokaj Aszú from Hungary
- Rutherglen Muscat from Australia.

Aromas, flavours and structure

These wines will often have a lot of colour, so don't be put off by deep gold, orange or (in the case of the Muscat) brown liquid swirling around your glass. You'll notice the wine is viscous and clings to the glass, due to the high percentage of residual sugar present and, in the case of the Muscat, high alcohol. Sweetness is the thing you will notice most in these wines.

You'll probably find all of these wines smell delicious. The intensely concentrated flavours should leap out of the glass. The Sauternes wine will have honeyed, lemony and floral aromas. As the wine gets older, the aromas will move towards the spectrum of butterscotch and caramel. You will probably also detect some bitter, orange peel-type notes to the smell. This is the effect of botrytis, the beneficial rot that affects Sauternes grapes and makes the wine taste so good. The wine will taste rich and sweet, with similar flavours to the aromas. It should have balanced acidity that is not too pronounced.

Botrytis is also a feature of the Tokaj wine, which will probably have a more pronounced bitter aroma. There is less of the honey character in this wine, as the varieties of grapes used to make it are different. The Tokaj will have a noticeable vein of acidity running through it. This is a much firmer style of wine than the other two, usually less generous and more mineral. The high acidity in this wine means that no matter how sweet it is, it is always fresh on the finish.

The Muscat will have aromas of toffee and raisins, maybe with a burnt caramel character. This will be the most lusciously sweet and highest in alcohol of the three wines. The sugar and alcohol give it a weighty, silky feel in the mouth. You will taste the grapey sweetness of the raisined berries used to make the wine. Notice how the acidity is probably much lower in this wine compared to the other two; the finish is softer and sweeter as a result.

Look out for sweet and luscious whites from:

- France: other Bordeaux wines (see Chapter 08); Alsace wines labelled 'Sélection de Grains Nobles'; Vins Doux Naturels from Muscat from the south; Jurançon; Vin de Paille
- Italy: Vin Santo; Recioto di Soave
- Spain: sweet (*dulce*) styles of sherry
- Germany: the sweetest categories of wine: Auslese, Beerenauslese, Trockenbeerenauslese and Eiswein
- Austria: from Neusiedlersee
- Portugal: sweeter Madeira wines: Bual and Malmsey
- South Africa: Constantia Muscat (vin de Constance)
- Canada: Ice wine.

Key red wine styles

Categorizing styles of red wine is a little trickier than for whites, because there are many possibilities of wine styles from the same grapes, regions and even producer. But the suggested tastings and groupings below should give you a good idea of the different styles of wine you can find, and help to make it easier to identify those you prefer. You'll notice that more of the wines here are included in several styles compared to the whites. For example, red wines from Bordeaux are classified as 'medium-bodied, crisp and tannic' for the lighter styles, and 'full-bodied and tannic' for the bigger, more age-worthy wines. Another influencing factor is the vintage, which can alter wine styles, especially in Europe. As a rule, you can expect more expensive red wines to have more concentrated flavours. These wines will often be aged in oak.

- light-bodied and fruity (page 115)
- medium-bodied, rich and supple (page 116)
- medium-bodied, crisp and tannic (page 117)
- full-bodied and fruity (page 119)
- full-bodied, firm and intense (page 120).

When choosing a style of red wine, here are some things to consider:

Do you prefer ...	Try these styles
fruity flavours?	light-bodied and fruity; medium-bodied, rich and supple; full-bodied and fruity
more savoury flavours?	medium-bodied, crisp and tannic; full-bodied, firm and intense
a quaffing wine for parties?	light-bodied and fruity
something to replace white wine?	light-bodied and fruity
wine with body that is not too dry?	medium-bodied, rich and supple
something not too strong in flavour?	light-bodied and fruity
oaky wines?	full-bodied and fruity; full-bodied, firm and intense
something to drink right away?	most wines, especially light-bodied and fruity; medium-bodied, rich and supple
something to keep?	full-bodied, firm and intense
wine with texture and weight?	full-bodied, firm and intense; full-bodied and fruity

Light-bodied and fruity

These wines are well suited for many occasions, as they tend to be lighter in tannins and alcohol than other red wines, so don't need to be drunk with food. These are also wines that will benefit from being chilled for summer drinking and are perfect for picnics and barbecues. You could think of them as a fuller-bodied alternative to a white wine. I've included rosé wines in this category.

Try these

- Rosé from the USA
- Sancerre (red) from France
- Beaujolais Villages from France
- Barbera from Argentina.

Wines in this style are lighter in colour and structure than other reds. They are low in tannins and feel light in the mouth, due to their moderate levels of alcohol. They have a structure that is more similar to white wines, with fresh fruit and crisp acidity. These are wines that are usually best drunk while they are young, alone or with food.

Aromas, flavours and structure

These wines will be more perfumed than most reds, with fresher, red fruit aromas and less obvious winemaking-type aromas, such as oak.

The American rosé will have soft, red fruit aromas and flavours. It will be relatively low in acidity and will probably taste slightly sweet. Its main flavours will be of juicy, red fruits.

The red Sancerre is made from the Pinot Noir grape, and will be quite pale in colour. The aromas will be also of red fruits, such as strawberries. The wine will feel light and refreshing on the palate, and will be completely dry, with a crisp finish.

Beaujolais wines are all made from the Gamay grape, which gives wines an upfront, fruity style. This wine will likely have a floral perfume, and possibly some bubblegum or boiled sweet aromas, the latter coming from the type of fermentation used to produce the wine. The flavours in the mouth will be of red and black fruits, often with a sweetness of fruit, although the wine will be dry. The fruity flavours will be quite crisp and light, and the level of alcohol moderate.

Barbera is from the north of Italy, but it is quite common in Argentina. Its wines have attractive, sour cherry aromas and flavours. Wines made from Barbera will always have good levels of acidity. From the warm climate of Argentina, Barbera gives juicy, plump fruit and a refreshing finish.

Look out for light and fruity reds and rosés from:

- France: Loire; Côtes du Rhône; Provence (rosé); Burgundy; Alsace; Champagne
- Italy: Veneto (Valpolicella); Piedmont (Barbera, Dolcetto)
- Spain: Navarra (rosé); lighter styles of Garnacha and Tempranillo
- USA: inexpensive California.

Medium-bodied, rich and supple

These are wines that will please most people, as they have soft, appealing fruit structure. As they are the kinds of wines people love, they are often at the higher price levels. These are good wines to serve at a family gathering or a special occasion, as they are likely to please young and old alike.

Try these

- Pinot Noir from New Zealand
- Rioja Reserva from Spain
- Blend from Alentejo region, Portugal
- Aged tawny port.

Aromas, flavours and structure

These wines have a little more weight than the group above, and higher levels of tannin. The tannins are not drying, however, and there is a substantial weight of fruit, which means that the wines taste smooth and satisfying in the mouth.

The Pinot Noir will be strongly and deliciously aromatic, with fresh, red fruit flavours and probably a touch of toasty oak evident. In the mouth it will feel silky and smooth, with full flavours of forest fruits and probably some oak spice. Tannins will be present, but not overwhelming. The alcohol may be on the higher side of average, so the wine may seem a little warm in the mouth. The crisp acidity on the finish will ensure that the wine will not appear overblown.

The aged Rioja wine will certainly have some oaky aromas, but the oak should not be harsh in the mouth. Instead, it will impart a soft, vanilla flavour to the wine. Here you can expect aromas and flavours of strawberries and spice. Everything about this wine is gentle and rounded, which is why so many people love it. Compared to the New Zealand Pinot Noir, you'll notice that this wine has much lower acidity.

The Alentejo blend will be full of ripe, fleshy fruit, with easy-going tannins and acidity. Flavours and aromas will depend on the varieties used, but you may find similar characteristics to the Rioja if the blend includes Aragonez, which is the local name for the main grape of Rioja, Tempranillo. Alentejo wines frequently display flavours of raspberries, chocolate and spice. The sunny climate produces reliably ripe wines with sweet fruit.

Tawny port is not a wine you're going to be serving every day, but it can be a delicious and special end to a meal with cheese or ice cream and can also be enjoyed served chilled as an aperitif. This will be quite different from the other wines, as it is fortified and sweet. It will have enticing aromas and flavours of raisins and nuts. Older wine will have delicious, evolved, complex flavours and softened acidity. There are some tannins evident, but these will mostly have been mellowed by the wine's ageing in oak. The finish will be long and warm.

Look out for medium-bodied, rich and supple reds from:

- France: aged Burgundy; Loire Valley; Côtes du Rhône; other southern Rhône; Cru Beaujolais; modern Vins de Pays from the south; Merlot-based wines from the south west
- Italy: Dolcetto from Piedmont; Salice Salentino and other reds from the south
- Austria
- Germany: Pinot Noir
- Any new world country: Pinot Noir
- Inexpensive, unoaked wines from Chile, Argentina, USA
- Spain: many wines from regions including Toro, Somontano, Campo de Borja.

Medium-bodied, crisp and tannic

These wines are more common in Europe than in the new world because European wines are more characterized by their structure than their ripeness of fruit. They have significant levels of tannins and acidity, but are not characterized by a full weight of fruit on the palate. These are wines you probably won't want to drink without food, as they can be quite drying in the mouth. They are versatile with food, though, as their refreshing acidity and medium weight make them an easy drink to choose. Many traditional wines fall into this category.

Try these

- Cabernet Sauvignon from Languedoc, France
- Chianti from Tuscany, Italy
- Premier Cru Burgundy (from Nuits-St-Georges, for example) from France
- Crozes-Hermitage from northern Rhône, France.

Aromas, flavours and structure

This selection is from four different grape varieties that can be made in styles that are lighter or heavier than this in other places. Here, the style is determined principally by the climate of the region where the grapes are grown. In a warmer climate, the grapes used to make these wines would yield riper flavours and higher levels of alcohol, which would make for a richer style.

The Languedoc Cabernet will be dark purple in colour and have distinctive blackcurranty, Cabernet Sauvignon fruit character. The structure will be crisp and tannic, with none of the richness and ripeness that one might find from Cabernet grown in a warmer climate, such as Australia. You might even taste some leafy greenness, especially if the vintage was not a ripe one. These characters will give it an austerity that marks it as being from a cooler climate. Notice how the wine feels in your mouth (probably quite dry).

The Chianti wine will be paler in colour than the Cabernet, as it is made predominantly or entirely from the paler-skinned, Sangiovese grape. You will be struck by the tannins in this wine, which are always dense and dry. The wine has high acidity. There should be a good weight of bright, sour cherry, plummy, leathery fruit flavours to balance the firm structure.

Burgundy is made from Pinot Noir, a grape with low levels of tannin. But a young example of Burgundy wine from good quality grapes grown on a top vineyard site (labelled Premier or Grand Cru) will show considerable crisp acidity and tannins, compared to its relatively restrained weight of fruit. (A new world Pinot Noir, in contrast, will usually show softer and sweeter, more immediately approachable fruit.) The flavours and structure of this wine will vary greatly according to the vintage and the person who made the wine, as Pinot Noir is a sensitive grape variety.

The wine from Crozes-Hermitage in the northern Rhône is made wholly from Syrah grapes. This wine has black fruit aromas similar to the Cabernet Sauvignon wine, but they probably have a sweeter edge. The flavours are of rich black fruits, leather and black pepper, and the structure will be firm but not unyielding. The fruit profile of Syrah is fleshier than Cabernet and Sangiovese, but in this relatively cool spot the wines are only of medium body.

Look out for medium-bodied, crisp and tannic reds from:

- France: Bordeaux and south west France; the Loire Valley; other less expensive northern Rhône (St Joseph, Cornas)
- Portugal: Douro, Dão, Bairrada
- Italy: centre and north (e.g. Barolo, Barbaresco, Barbera, Montepulciano)
- Greece
- New Zealand: Bordeaux blends (Cabernet/Merlot)
- Spain: Cabernet Sauvignon from Navarra
- Eastern Europe
- USA: Washington
- South Africa
- Australia: Shiraz from Hunter Valley.

Full-bodied and fruity

These are wines that are defined by their fruit. This style is more likely to come from the new world than the old, since in the new world it is easier to make wines with juicy, upfront fruit and full flavours. However, this full-bodied, fruity style is also common in warmer parts of Europe. These are easy-going wines that do not demand food, but due to their often higher-than-average alcohol levels, it's probably a good idea to eat when drinking them. Their full flavours are generally much appreciated, although for people who don't like their wine to taste too strong, these may be a little overwhelming.

Try these

- Zinfandel (red, not pink) from California
- Primitivo from Italy
- Malbec from Argentina
- Shiraz from McLaren Vale, Australia.

Aromas, flavour and structure

These wines will all be predominantly fruity in the mouth. The ripeness of the fruit will balance any impression of harshness from tannins or acidity.

In California, the Zinfandel grape variety produces wines that taste of sweet, ripe fruit. Zinfandel wines typically have a sweet, raisined character, and flavours ranging from plums to chocolate and cherries. The structure of this wine is soft, with low levels of tannins and acidity, but the alcohol is usually high and noticeable.

In America, the simple, upfront fruit of Zinfandel makes it a popular barbecue wine.

Italy's Primitivo is quite different: typically it is deeply coloured, full and spicy, with black fruit character and more of a dark chocolate bitterness to the fruit. Since it is grown in the warm south of the country, the wine will reflect the fully ripe grapes. This is a full-bodied and rich, but entirely approachable style that is easily appreciated.

A good quality Malbec from Argentina will show lots of vibrant fruit and fairly low levels of tannin. However, it may appear tannic from being aged in oak or from being blended with another, more tannic variety, such as Cabernet Sauvignon. The fruit is rich, rounded and supple, and alcohol is often above 14 per cent. Malbec is typically a big, fruity mouthful, often perfumed with violets and spice.

Shiraz from McLaren Vale is one of Australia's richest, most intense styles, with dense, dark fruit character. This wine will be deep in colour, with a peppery, blackcurrant nose. The palate will have juicy, ripe, full-bodied fruit, with an opulence verging on chocolate. This weight of fruit covers the big but silky tannic structure of this wine.

Other full-bodied and fruity reds to look out for:

- France: Châteauneuf-du-Pape; Grenache-based sweet wines from the south
- USA: Cabernet Sauvignon from Napa; other top-quality reds from California
- South Africa: Pinotage, Merlot
- Australia: Grenache and Grenache blends
- Chile: good quality Carmenère and Syrah/Shiraz
- New Zealand: Syrah/Shiraz.

Full-bodied, firm and intense

This style of wine is found in the new world or the old world. These wines are characterized by their concentration and structure, which means they are, by definition, wines that can age well. They are often expensive because of this. Most of these wines will need some time in bottle to soften before they are ready to drink. If you drink them young they will taste tannic, hard and dry. Over time, the fruit will open up, the tannins will mellow and they will become complex wines to sip and enjoy.

They are not wines to drink in a hurry, in a pub, or anywhere standing up. A mature example of one of these wines is one of the most satisfying and enjoyable drinks you will find.

Try these
- Hermitage from the northern Rhône, France
- Cabernet Sauvignon from Napa Valley, USA
- Amarone della Valpolicella from Italy
- Young vintage port from Portugal.

Aromas, flavour and structure

The top wines of the northern Rhône are powerful examples of the Syrah grape. This Hermitage wine will be fragrant, with aromas of blackcurrants, pepper and oak spice. In the mouth it will probably taste quite dry and may be unapproachable if it is young. If this is the case, try to focus on what is going on underneath the tannins. You should find a good concentration of ripe, black fruit character. Notice the length of flavour of this wine. If you are lucky enough to find a wine with a few years' age, you will find intense fruit flavours, enveloping but softened tannins and a long finish.

The Cabernet Sauvignon from California's Napa Valley, if it is a good example, will be an age-worthy red with full, rich, dark fruit character and probably quite noticeable oak. Even though they have the ample tannins found in all Cabernet Sauvignon wines, Napa Cabernets are often drunk young. This is because they benefit from a warm, sunny climate and a high level of modern winemaking expertise, both of which ensure that the wines are approachably ripe, full-bodied and fruity. The fruit is to the fore from the start, unlike the Hermitage, where it may take time to come out. This wine will probably be powerful and concentrated in flavour, with lush ripeness, black fruit character and a firm weight of tannins from both the fruit and the oak. On the finish, you will probably taste the sweetness of the fruit and a touch of warmth from the alcohol.

Amarone wine is made from semi-dried grapes. This process concentrates all the flavours and makes for a firm and long-lived wine that is barely recognizable as sharing the raw material of light, cherry-scented Valpolicella. Amarone is a deeply coloured wine with intense, raisined, black cherry, chocolatey aromas and a palate often verging on sweet but with a bitter finish. This is high in alcohol (15 per cent, or more), but due to the amazing concentration of the wine, it can still taste balanced.

Vintage port is one of the most tannic of wines, made from grapes baked in the heat of the Douro Valley. It can take decades for this style of port to soften to the point it tastes smooth and balanced, but some aficionados prefer the vigour and power of fruit it shows in its youth. Sweet, high in alcohol and tannins and richly flavoured, this is one of the most intense full-bodied wines.

Other full-bodied, firm and intense reds to look out for:

- France: Côte Rôtie from the northern Rhône; Madiran from the south west; some Roussillon wines
- Italy: 'SuperTuscans' from Bolgheri; some styles of Barolo; Brunello di Montalcino
- Spain: Ribera del Duero, Priorat
- Australia: Cabernet Sauvignon from Coonawarra or Margaret River.

08

wine regions: Europe

In this chapter you will learn:
- which are the most important wine-producing countries of Europe
- which regions to look out for and the styles of wine they produce
- which wines you should try to get a better understanding of the producing regions of Europe.

It's hard to find a country that doesn't make at least some wine these days. And not only is there more wine, there is more good wine than ever before. Advances in understanding of grape growing and winemaking, together with the globalization of wine knowledge have led to experimentation in areas where viticulture was previously unknown. This chapter and the next outline the main areas where wine is made and the wines you can expect to find there.

Top wine-producing countries	Millions of bottles
1 France	7652
2 Italy	7067
3 Spain	5732
4 USA	2680
5 Argentina	2062
6 Australia	1842
7 China	1560
8 Germany	1340
9 South Africa	1237
10 Portugal	998
Total world production	39,756

Source: OIV. Figures are for 2004 and are rounded. Quantity shown is equivalent total production expressed as 75 cl bottles.

The wines of Europe still dominate the world map in terms of both quantity and quality. The top four producing countries in Europe – France, Spain, Italy and Germany – between them account for over half of the world's wine production. Europe tends to be referred to as the old world when it comes to producing wine, but as winemaking techniques and winemakers travel the globe, this is a distinction that is becoming increasingly blurred.

The greatest difference between the wines of Europe and those of the new world is vintage. Vintage matters a lot in Europe and a lot less in the new world. If you try a wine from Europe that you don't like, it may be entirely the fault of the poor weather at the harvest time. In the best vintages, though, most producers should be making good wine. If you try a top vintage and still don't like the wine, then it's time to blame the winemaker.

France

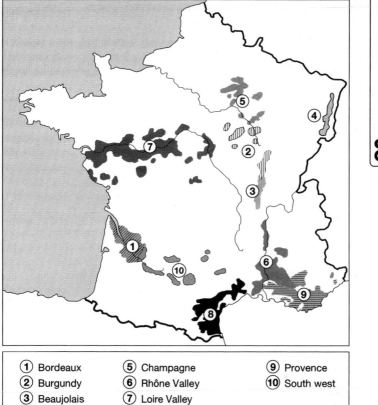

① Bordeaux	⑤ Champagne	⑨ Provence
② Burgundy	⑥ Rhône Valley	⑩ South west
③ Beaujolais	⑦ Loire Valley	
④ Alsace	⑧ Languedoc-Roussillon	

figure 8.1 wine regions in France

It is faced by stiff competition on many fronts, but France is still the most important wine-producing nation in the world today. Apart from the fact that it regularly produces more wine than any other country, its most famous wines remain the benchmarks for the rest of the world. Champagne, red Bordeaux, red and white Burgundy, and the red wines of the northern Rhône are the models for many of the wines produced from the 'international' varieties of Cabernet Sauvignon, Pinot Noir, Chardonnay and Syrah in other countries.

France at a glance

World's largest wine-producing country; some 350 AOC/AC (Appellation d'Origine Contrôlée) regions.

Bordeaux – France's best-known and largest fine wine region, famous for its elegant red blends from Cabernet Sauvignon and Merlot and whites (sweet and dry) from Sauvignon Blanc and Sémillon.

Burgundy (includes Chablis) – Most wines from single varietals: reds from Pinot Noir, whites from Chardonnay.

Beaujolais – Officially part of Burgundy, though stylistically closer to Rhône wines from further south. Early drinking, fruity reds, 100 per cent from the Gamay grape, predominate. The best wines are from the ten 'Cru' villages (see Chapter 03). A tiny amount of white wine is made from Chardonnay.

Alsace – Fullish, single varietal wines, almost all white, from Riesling, Pinot Gris, Gewurztraminer, Sylvaner, Pinot Blanc and Muscat grapes. Light reds from Pinot Noir.

Champagne – The world's favourite sparkling wine.

Rhône Valley – Mostly generous reds based around Syrah (in the north) and Grenache (in the south), but some noteworthy whites as well.

Loire Valley – Best region for dry whites from Sauvignon Blanc, and Chenin Blanc, the latter at all levels of sweetness. Lots of sparkling wine and some notable reds from Cabernet Franc.

Languedoc-Roussillon – Large Mediterranean region, with some good value and individual wines, plus many single varietal wines from international grape varieties.

Provence – Best known for its dry and refreshing, often full-bodied rosés, which account for over 80 per cent of the wine produced here.

South west – Many characterful wines for early consumption in all colours. Those closest to Bordeaux often use the same grape varieties. Further south, in the Basque country, some original wines from more unusual grapes are to be found.

Bordeaux

Probably the most famous wine name in the world, Bordeaux is France's largest fine wine region. Situated in the south-west of the country, around the city of Bordeaux on the Gironde estuary, it has a damp, maritime climate that favours the production of medium-bodied red wines. These are made principally from Cabernet Sauvignon and Merlot, and a lesser amount of Cabernet Franc. A good proportion of the wine is white, both sweet and dry. Dry whites are from Sauvignon Blanc and Sémillon, while sweet whites are made from late-harvested Sémillon and Sauvignon Blanc grapes.

There are 57 different appellations in the Bordeaux region. The red wines are the most celebrated. Those on the Bordeaux side of the Gironde estuary, the 'Left Bank', are mainly Cabernet Sauvignon based, since only here are the conditions warm enough to ripen this grape variety fully; those on the much larger 'Right Bank' are mainly Merlot-dominant blends. Like many great wine regions, the climate here is marginal for the varieties of grapes that are grown. To compensate for deficiencies in ripening the different varieties, the wines from Bordeaux have traditionally always been blended, and this is still the case today.

Bordeaux's best red wines come from a small number of appellations. On the Left Bank these are: St-Estèphe, Pauillac, St-Julien, Margaux and Pessac-Léognan (the last is also the area where the best dry whites are found). On the Right Bank, the two best appellations for quality are St-Emilion and Pomerol. For cheaper examples look for wines labelled 'Médoc' and 'Haut-Médoc' on the Left Bank. Wines from the Right Bank communes surrounding Saint-Emilion that feature the famous village in their names can offer better value than wines from Saint-Emilion.

Bordeaux can produce the best expression of a Cabernet-Merlot blend anywhere, and every level of wine from the top down. If you find the cheaper end of the market uninspiring, you are not alone. Unfortunately, quality is not consistently good throughout the region, due in part to the variable climate and also the fact that some producers have been slow to react to the growing competition from warmer countries that can produce ripe, fresh wines year in, year out.

Try these

Quality and style comparisons to try for Bordeaux reds.

- AC Bordeaux wine – light in structure, probably Merlot-based, early drinking style
- AC Saint-Emilion Grand Cru – deeper in colour, with more concentrated flavours of blackcurrants, plums and smoky oak; structure quite noticeable
- AC Haut-Médoc or Pauillac – deep in colour, like AC Saint-Emilion Grand Cru, with more obvious tannins that feel drier in the mouth; still has blackcurrant and cassis flavours, but probably less juicy, less weighty, less smooth compared to the second wine.

The dry whites of Bordeaux can range from inexpensive, bland, soft Sémillons and Sauvignon Blancs to sumptuous, dry, oaked blends of the same varieties, transformed by site, care and attention. The best dry whites of Bordeaux can cost as much as the top red wines. If you enjoy dry, oaked whites, look out for these wines, which can age as well as white Burgundy wines. White wine vintages are more consistent than red wine vintages in Bordeaux, although the trend towards higher average temperatures during the growing season means that all wines from Bordeaux are more reliably ripe than they were even ten years ago.

Try these

Quality and style comparison to try for dry Bordeaux whites.

- AC Bordeaux Sauvignon Blanc – pale in colour, clean and fresh, but less crisp and zesty, and with milder character than a Sauvignon from the Loire Valley or New Zealand
- AC Pessac-Léognan – probably has noticeable, oaky aromas; most likely to be a blend of Sauvignon Blanc and Semillon, which will give the wine extra weight in the mouth, more waxy, lanolin, lemony flavours, and a longer finish.

The best-known sweet wines of the region are those of Sauternes, which produces the finest quality the most often. The appellation includes the neighbouring village of Barsac, which you may find mentioned alone on a wine label, being also of excellent quality. Other less expensive, but good sweet wine appellations to look out for are Ste-Croix-du-Mont, Loupiac and Premières Côtes de Bordeaux.

Burgundy

Burgundy is the home of Pinot Noir and Chardonnay, but it is for its Pinot Noir that it is particularly renowned, because unlike Chardonnay, which grows successfully all over the place, Pinot Noir is rather fussier. There are very few places that can produce grapes to compare to the quality of Pinot Noir grown in Burgundy, and there is certainly nowhere that has the history of fine wine production of Burgundy. You could drink quite a lot of red Burgundy and still wonder what all the fuss is about, though, since none of it is cheap and much of it is mediocre.

Like Bordeaux, Burgundy is another region that is a marginal climate for the grapes grown, so the red wines (in particular) vary in quality from year to year. The white wines are more reliable in quality, since the grapes ripen at cooler temperatures. The real secret of enjoying Burgundy, though, is to know the name of the producer on the bottle.

Try these

Quality and style comparison to try for Burgundy whites – all made from 100 per cent Chardonnay.

- AC Chablis (or AC Chablis Premier Cru) – expect mineral, slatey, non-fruit flavours here; will be crisp and light and lean in style
- AC Bourgogne Blanc – the basic appellation for white Burgundy; will probably be easy-drinking, with mild, lemony notes, perhaps some mineral flavours and good acidity
- AC Pouilly-Fuissé/Mâcon/St-Véran – more full-bodied style, perhaps with some creamy oak influence; weightier and richer than the other two, less mineral and less crisp
- AC Meursault/Puligny-Montrachet – these top appellations should show greater depth of flavour and, more than likely, toasty oak notes. Meursault will have a nutty richness, while Puligny-Montrachet will combine intense mineral flavours with racy acidity; both should have more persistent length than the other three wines.

Try these

Quality and style comparison to try for Burgundy reds – all made from 100 per cent Pinot Noir.

- AC Bourgogne Pinot Noir – light in colour and weight, with red fruit aromas
- AC Volnay – light colour, more pronounced floral aromas, firmer tannins, delicate but full-flavoured
- AC Nuits-St-Georges/Gevrey-Chambertin/Chambolle-Musigny/Vosne-Romanée – deeper colour than the previous two wines, with aromas that may range from black and red fruits to earthy, mineral and medicinal; fuller in the mouth than the previous two wines, with more obvious weight and power.

Alsace

Alsace sits apart from the other fine wine regions of France, both geographically and stylistically. Single varietal wines are what Alsace is all about and almost all are white. This makes it a lot easier to understand the wines, just as long as you are familiar with the varieties in question (if in doubt, refer to Chapter 03). This is the only place in the country where a wine that is labelled 'Grand Cru' will also state the name of the grape variety on the bottle. The major grape varieties you'll find from Alsace are Riesling, Gewurztraminer, Pinot Gris, Muscat, Pinot Blanc, Pinot Noir (the only black grape) and Sylvaner.

In style, the white wines are riper and more full-bodied than one might expect, given the northerly location of the vineyards, but they still retain good crispness and balance. Most of the wines are dry, often with austere, mineral flavours, but they can range in sweetness from bone dry to richly sweet. The term Sélection de Grains Nobles, meaning that the wine has been produced from selected grapes affected by noble rot, indicates that the wine will be sweet, as does the term Vendanges Tardives (late harvest – although, confusingly, these wines can also be dry). Beyond this, it is the major drawback of Alsace wines that one usually doesn't know if the wine will be slightly sweet before the bottle is opened, so it is always worth checking if the person you are buying from has done his or her homework to provide this information for you. The level of sweetness in the wines is less a function of the vintage than the belief of the producer whether the wine should be dry or not!

Alsace produces world-class white wines. Rieslings are mineral, (usually) dry and intense in flavour; Pinot Gris can be rich, honeyed, mineral, and sweet or dry; Gewurztraminer comes in a range of styles, but always with heady intensity of aroma and full weight of fruit on the palate. Muscats from Alsace are fairly rare, but make a deliciously fragrant, dry aperitif. Pinot Blanc and Sylvaner make refreshing, lighter styles. Pinot Noirs are of less interest than the whites and, perhaps because of their relative scarcity, are usually expensive. There is also a fair amount of sparkling, Crémant wine made here from a blend of the white varieties.

Try these

Alsace tastings to try:

- Try several different varieties to see if you can taste a distinctive Alsace character in all of them.
- Try two wines each from two producers to get an idea of differences in house style.
- Try one variety made in different styles – Pinot Gris, Gewurztraminer or Riesling make good late-harvest, sweeter wines.

Champagne

'Real' Champagne can only come from the Champagne region of France: the Champenois have fought long and hard to protect the name of the world's most famous sparkling wine. It's probably the most imitated of France's wines, but nowhere else has come remotely close to replicating its success for quality sparkling wine production, due to the region's unique combination of chalky soil, cool, northern climate and skilful marketing.

The wines can be made from three permitted grape varieties: Pinot Noir and Pinot Meunier (both black-skinned grapes) and Chardonnay. Most wines are blends of these grapes, pressed so gently that no colour is transmitted from the skins into the juice. Some Champagnes are made only from the black grapes and will be labelled Blanc de Noirs (which means white wine from black grapes). Champagne made only from Chardonnay will be labelled Blanc de Blancs.

Champagne is the one region of France with many well-known brand names. Most of the wine is non-dated, or non-vintage, being a blend of several years' wines. This is done to maintain a consistency of style. In very good vintages (of which there are more and more, it seems), producers will release vintage-dated wines, which are aged for longer and which sell for far higher prices. A small amount of still red wine is made in Champagne.

Try these

Champagne tastings to try:

- Compare a vintage and non-vintage Champagne from the same producer.
- Try a blind sparkling wine tasting with some friends. See if anyone can spot the Champagne.

Rhône Valley

The Rhône Valley is usually divided into north and south. The north is best known for its outstanding red wines made almost exclusively from the Syrah grape. These ripe, but peppery and somewhat restrained wines provide the reference for fine wines from Syrah (or Shiraz, as it is also known) throughout the world. Syrah is the only black grape you need to know about for the wines of the northern Rhône: it's the only one allowed. The top red wine appellations in the northern Rhône are Hermitage and Côte Rôtie, followed by Crozes-Hermitage, St-Joseph and Cornas.

The climate dictates that white wines are in the minority in the Rhône Valley. The most notable whites come from the north, named after the local town of Condrieu. These are fragrant, full-bodied and usually delicious wines, invariably dry and made exclusively from the Viognier grape. Condrieu sets the standard for quality wine from Viognier in the world. Other whites, from the Marsanne and Roussanne grapes, are dry and full-bodied, with herb-tinged, savoury flavours.

Try these

A tasting of northern Rhône wines:

- AC Crozes-Hermitage white – herbal and savoury and full in the mouth
- AC Condrieu – perfumed and rich white wine, with silky texture and full weight of fruit
- AC Crozes-Hermitage red – often good value, this is a Syrah with supple structure but none of the sweet fruit of new world examples of this grape
- AC Hermitage – top-notch Syrah; notice the intensity of perfume and the firm, but not unyielding structure; can taste of blackcurrants, black pepper, meat and leather.

Further south, the warmer climate is evident in the wines, which are more generous, with sweeter flavours and higher levels of alcohol. In this larger, more diverse region, a broad mix of grape varieties can be found, and there are many different appellations. Perhaps the best known wines from the south are the ubiquitous and easy-drinking Côtes du Rhône wines and the smoothly serious reds of Châteauneuf-du-Pape. The most commonly encountered grape of the southern Rhône is Grenache, which is present in all the reds. Most often, it is blended with one or more other varieties, including Syrah, Mourvèdre and Cinsault. There are many good value wines with real individuality in the southern Rhône. Look out for wines from the Côtes du Rhône-Villages (which come from the best villages in the vast Côtes du Rhône appellation), Lirac, Gigondas and Vacqueyras.

Try these

A tasting of southern Rhône wines:

- AC Côtes du Rhône – red and white – these easy, soft, gluggable wines are of reliable quality; for a step up, try Côtes du Rhône-Villages wines
- AC Cairanne – one of the best villages in the Côtes du Rhône, Cairanne makes concentrated, juicy wines of considerable elegance
- AC Rasteau – powerful, rich and often alcoholic, Grenache-based wine
- AC Châteauneuf-du-Pape – smooth and complex, often oaky, easy to enjoy fairly young, but also long-lived.

Loire Valley

If you consider that the Loire is the longest river in France, it's not surprising that the vineyards of the Loire Valley are so spread out, extending westwards from Sancerre in central France to the coast at Nantes. Every style of wine is made along this stretch of vineyards that is often said to mark the climatic divide between the north and the south of the country. But although they are diverse in terms of colour, sweetness and grape varieties, the wines of the Loire Valley share several common characteristics. They are all marked by the effects of a cool climate, at a latitude of 47 degrees north. All have crisp acidity and are medium-bodied (high levels of alcohol are rare here). And most are made from a single grape variety.

Due to its northern locality, the most successful wines of the Loire Valley are white. The main grape varieties are Sauvignon Blanc (the grape of Sancerre and Pouilly Fumé), Chenin Blanc (which makes Vouvray, Anjou Blanc, Saumur and Coteaux du Layon) and Melon de Bourgogne (the grape of Muscadet). Dominant for red wines is Cabernet Franc, the minority Bordeaux grape that, when ripe, can produce deliciously fragrant, light, juicy reds that are usually best consumed young. Cabernet Franc makes the red wines of Chinon, Bourgeuil, Saumur and Saumur-Champigny.

Try these

Here are some must-try Loire whites:

- Sparkling wine – AC Saumur Brut – the Loire Valley's Champagne equivalent
- Sauvignon Blanc – AC Sancerre/Pouilly-Fumé/Quincy/Reuilly – crisp and fresh, grassy flavours
- Dry Chenin Blanc – AC Vouvray/Montlouis/Anjou Blanc – intense and often slightly bitter, with honeyed, apple flavours
- Sweet Chenin Blanc – AC Coteaux du Layon/Coteaux de l'Aubance/Bonnezeaux – ranging from medium-sweet to some of the most luscious wines in France, with Chenin's characteristic bitter, honeyed, 'wet wool' flavours

And some must-try Loire reds, all from the Cabernet Franc grape:

- AC Saumur-Champigny/Chinon/Bourgeuil/St Nicolas de Bourgeuil – fragrant, mid-weight wines, with quite dry tannins and good fruity freshness.

Languedoc-Roussillon and Provence

The far south of France is responsible for much anonymous plonk, but equally, some really exciting, flavourful wines that are as easy on the pocket as they are on the palate. These are wines with individual flavours of the south, ripe but not overripe, chunky but not heavy, and full without being over-alcoholic. Provence is renowned for its full-bodied, dry rosé. Roussillon specializes in the production of Vins Doux Naturels (or VDNs), wines that are fortified, sweet and intense. Reds are usually made from Grenache (for example, AC Banyuls or Maury), and whites from Muscat (such as Muscat de Rivesaltes).

Italy

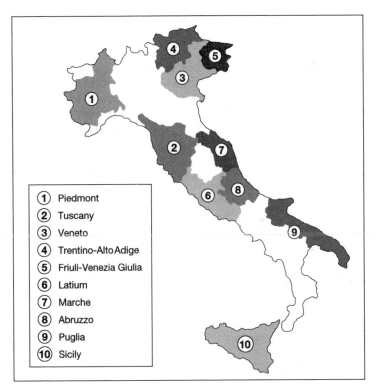

① Piedmont
② Tuscany
③ Veneto
④ Trentino-Alto Adige
⑤ Friuli-Venezia Giulia
⑥ Latium
⑦ Marche
⑧ Abruzzo
⑨ Puglia
⑩ Sicily

figure 8.2 wine regions in Italy

In volume terms, Italy is France's equal; for quality, its best wines equal the great wines of France. Yet Italy is a much harder country to define and to know. This is largely a question of grapes. In contrast to France's relatively familiar range of 'international' grape varieties that have been exported the world over, in Italy most of the grapes are local (sometimes very local) and so are the styles of wine they produce. Most Italian wines have no equivalent anywhere else in the world. Add to this singularity of raw material a good measure of Italian creativity and you have probably the world's most interesting wine nation.

Italy at a glance

Second largest producer. Well over 200 DOC (Denominazione di Origine Controllata) regions and some 40 DOCGs (Denominazione di Origine Controllata e Garantita) – the latter being the highest rating in the system.

Piedmont – Home of Italy's most acclaimed reds from Nebbiolo (from the towns of Barolo and Barbaresco) and sparkling Moscato from Asti; other important grape names to look for are Barbera and Dolcetto – both red (see Chapter 03 for more on these varieties).

Veneto – Mostly light, quaffing wines from Soave (white) and Valpolicella (light red); some excellent sweet and dry dried grape wines from both: Recioto di Soave (bittersweet white) and Amarone della Valpolicella (rich, dry red).

Trentino-Alto Adige – Interesting, pristine, aromatic whites, especially Gewurztraminer, from this cool area in Italy's far north. For reds, try the fruity wines from the Teroldego grape.

Friuli-Venezia Giulia – Highly regarded, food-friendly, dry whites, not in a blockbuster style.

Tuscany – best known for wines based around the Sangiovese grape, which has many synonyms. Key places to look for on the label: Chianti, Montalcino, Montepulciano. Interesting (and pricey) wines from blends of Sangiovese and Bordeaux grape varieties from the coast at Bolgheri.

Other central regions – These include Latium (home of dry, buttery white, Frascati), Marche (try the lemony whites from the Verdicchio grape), Abruzzo (home of the soft and plummy black grape, Montepulciano) and Molise.

Puglia, Sicily and the south – Reds of Italy's south are big and mouthfilling, with black fruit flavours and more noticeable levels of alcohol. Look for wines made from Negroamaro, Primitivo and Aglianico. Some very good wines from Nero d'Avola in Sicily.

Every one of Italy's 20 regions produces wine. You could spend a lifetime discovering the thousands of individual wines this country produces. To make things simpler, below are the styles of wine you can expect to find there.

Italian whites

Italy's best-known white wines hail mainly from the north of the country. Sparkling Prosecco and Franciacorta offer a light and savoury, good value aperitif wine. Still white wine is made in the north, including the ubiquitous Soave and hugely popular Pinot Grigio. Usually dry, they are crisp and light enough to be refreshing, yet rarely very high in acidity, nor strong in flavour or aroma. This makes them a popular choice with restaurants and bars, as they are easy to drink with or without food. There are good Italian whites from all over the country that show similar characters – light to medium in body, often with creamy, almondy, peach and lemon flavours and an appealing savoury, bitter character. If you move up the quality scale, you will find that the wines have more concentrated flavours, usually due to lower yields (rather than oak ageing). Commonly, the wines have strong mineral character and often a characteristic bitter finish. The north of the country is recognized as the source of Italy's best, most minerally white wines. Increasingly, Italian winemakers are blending their indigenous varieties with international grapes such as Chardonnay, but don't let this deter you from buying the wines made from Italian grapes, which can provide delicious, original, 100 per cent Italian flavours.

Try these

Interesting white wines to try from Italy:

- Verdicchio dei Castelli di Jesi Classico DOC – crisp and refreshing, light and lemon-scented white with a bitter, lemon zest twist at the finish
- Roero Arneis DOCG – herbal and intense wine from Piedmont, with ripe, almost tropical flavours
- Fiano di Avellino DOCG – a wine of good intensity and medium to full body, with savoury, mineral and peardrop characters
- Gewurztraminer from Trentino Alto Adige – perfumed, light and elegant – an ethereal and delicious wine
- Vernaccia di San Gimignano DOCG – crisp, medium-bodied and round, with appealing nutty character.

Italian reds

Italy has a fabulous and often confusing array of red wines and it is here that the best of Italy is to be found. Styles range from immediately quaffable, pale reds to highly tannic, dry wines that need long ageing. As a generalization, Italian reds are medium-bodied, with moderate alcohol and crisp acidity. Compared to French reds, they are more reliably ripe in flavour, although commonly found flavours such as plums or cherries can give an impression of sourness. Many Italian grape varieties are high in tannins, which will make the wines taste quite dry in the mouth. There is also usually some degree of bitterness to all Italian wines – even those made with international varieties – which marks them out as being distinctly Italian. This combination of characters makes Italian reds more suited to drinking with food than without.

Try these

Easy drinking Italian reds to try:

- Valpolicella DOC – light and bright, crisp and cherry-flavoured
- Dolcetto d'Alba DOC – plenty of colour and fruit, noticeable tannins, but softer acidity than most Italian reds
- Nero d'Avola from Sicily – soft, plummy fruit
- Salice Salentino DOC – generous, warm, black fruits predominate here
- Montepulciano d'Abruzzo DOCG – soft, easy, quaffing wine.

For a step up, try these:

- Cerasuolo di Vittoria DOCG – lightweight but full in flavour, this Sicilian red made principally from the Nero d'Avola grape has ripe, cherry and strawberry flavours
- Chianti and Chianti Classico DOCG – firmly structured, with high levels of tannin and acidity, and savoury, ripe fruit with flavours of plums and leather
- Rosso di Montalcino DOC – another Sangiovese wine, like the Chianti, with good richness and weight
- Barbera d'Alba DOC – bright and fresh, with zingy acidity and cherry fruitiness.

And if you like those, try these – the giants of Italy that will need a few years in bottle before drinking:

- Barolo DOCG – intense wine, with exotic, often floral, perfume and complex flavours, which take time to evolve; high levels of tannin can make it unapproachable when young

- Barbaresco DOCG – the same grape variety as Barolo (Nebbiolo), Barbaresco wines are distinguished by their elegance and slightly lighter character
- Brunello di Montalcino DOCG – one of the finest expressions of Sangiovese, with balance and structure and powerful, rich flavours
- Amarone della Valpolicella DOC – firm, highly flavoured dried grape wine that transforms the naturally light grapes of Valpolicella; wines have high alcohol and flavours of raisins, chocolate and cherries.

Dried grape wines

Italy is home to many historic dried grape wines, both sweet and dry. These wines have extra-concentrated flavours because they are made from ripe grapes that have been allowed to shrivel, thereby losing water. They were probably born from a desire to make more interesting wines with less interesting grapes. Due to the extra cost involved in making them (and the necessarily lower quantities), they do tend to be more expensive.

Try this

Dried-grape wine to try:

- Amarone della Valpolicella (dry red) DOC (see above).

Spain

This traditional winegrowing country has been undergoing an exciting renaissance in recent years. While the sherries and older-style, cask-aged reds that made Spain's name are still plentiful, you are now just as likely to find zesty, modern whites and vibrant young reds, not to mention an abundance of fruity rosé and good value Cava when you shop for Spanish wine.

Spain at a glance

Third largest producer. 65 DOs (Denominación de Origen), 2 DOCas (Denominación de Origen Calificada).

Rioja – The most important and best known of Spain's regions. The best wines are the supple, strawberry- and vanilla-scented reds, based around the indigenous Tempranillo grape. Variable, often oaky, whites.

Ribera del Duero – Fashionable, expensive, high-quality, intense reds from Tempranillo. Firmer than Rioja in style.

Rías Baixas – Source of Spain's best whites, from the Albariño grape.

Toro – Juicy, youthful reds from Grenache and Tempranillo.

Rueda – Crisp, easy whites from Verdejo and Sauvignon Blanc.

Somontano/Campo de Borja/Calatayud/Cariñena – Good, fresh, uncomplicated wines with upfront fruit.

Priorat – Concentrated, tannic and expensive Grenache-based reds from this relatively new region, which recently became only the second Denominación de Origen Calificada (DOCa), alongside Rioja.

Navarra – Plentiful source of rosé, principally from Garnacha, plus reds from Tempranillo and international varieties.

Penedès – Best known for Cava sparkling wines.

Jerez – Sherry.

Spanish whites

If you've drunk much Spanish white wine in the past, you probably remember it as tasting mainly of oak, since the traditional way of making both reds and whites was to age the wines for long periods in oak. These wines still do exist (stick with Rioja and you'll soon find them), but today you are more likely to find white wines with little or no oak that are both fruity and refreshing. Drink them young and you won't be disappointed. The most interesting grape varieties to look out for are Albariño and Verdejo. Albariño is produced in the north-west of the country and makes fresh, apricot- and peach-scented whites. These are arguably the best dry whites of Spain, though general recognition of this fact has pushed the price up lately. Verdejo is a grape from the Rueda region, north-west of Madrid. It makes wines that are crisp, green and attractive, somewhat reminiscent of Sauvignon Blanc in character and usually good value for money.

① Rías Baixas	⑤ Rioja	⑨ Calatayud	⑬ Jerez
② Toro	⑥ Navarra	⑩ Somontano	
③ Rueda	⑦ Campo de Borja	⑪ Priorat	
④ Ribera del Duero	⑧ Cariñena	⑫ Penedès	

figure 8.3 wine regions in Spain

Try these

Must-try Spanish whites:

- Albariño from Rías Baixas
- Verdejo from Rueda
- White Rioja.

Spanish reds

Spanish red wines are characterized by their open, soft fruitiness and, often, vanilla and oak flavours. Compared to France and Italy, the flavours of Spanish wine are generally riper and sweeter, with smooth tannins and acidities. This makes them exceptionally good crowd pleasers in the same way that new world wines are so immediately appealing. The wines are very often based on the native Garnacha grape (known as Grenache in other countries) and Tempranillo (the main grape of Rioja and Ribera del Duero, which has many synonyms throughout Spain). Most Spanish wine can be enjoyed when it is young – undoubtedly another reason for its popularity.

Try these

Must-try Spanish reds:

- Rioja is the most important region to try from Spain, but look out for other interesting reds from Navarra, Toro, Somontano, Ribera del Duero and Priorat.

Sherry

From the far south of Spain, these are fortified, aged wines from around the town of Jerez (from where we get the name sherry). Only wines from here may be sold as sherry. If you're not very familiar with sherry, you might remember it as a sweet drink forced upon you at Christmas by an ageing relation. But don't write sherry off. There is a lot more to it than this. Most 'real' sherry is actually dry. Once you try them, you'll realize that pale cream sherry has little in common with these wines. As well as an aperitif, dry sherry (especially the lightest, Fino style) is lovely to drink with food. Fino sherry (which includes Manzanilla) is a pale wine that is tangy, salty and yeasty in flavour, and always bone dry. Amontillado is darker, and aged for longer. It is richer, nutty in flavour, usually higher in alcohol and often slightly sweeter (though usually still dry). Oloroso (meaning 'scented') is darker still in colour, and will have higher alcohol again, though it is also dry. Also try PX if you get the chance. This is the thickest, richest, sweetest sherry of all, made from the Pedro Ximénez grape. You'll struggle to drink more than a small glass of this, but it is really very good, and also delicious poured on ice cream or as an accompaniment other desserts.

Try these

Must-try sherries:

- Fino or Manzanilla – drink chilled like any dry white wine or with salty snacks
- Amontillado – chilled or at room temperature, try it with cheese
- Dry Oloroso – dark, intense and dry, serve cool or at room temperature as a warming after-dinner drink with nuts or cheese
- Sweet Oloroso – serve cool with a nutty dessert, or on its own.

Germany

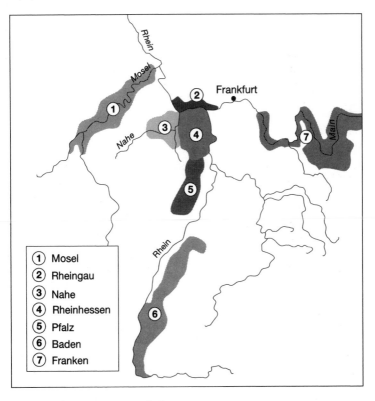

figure 8.4 Germany's wine-producing areas

Though to some extent still suffering from its image as a producer of cheap, low-quality, sweet white wines, German wine has taken off in interesting new directions in recent years. These days, German wine is as likely to be dry as it is sweet. If you want dry wine, look out for the word 'trocken' on the label. If there is no mention that the wine is dry, you can assume it will be off-dry or sweeter. Increasingly, we are likely to be seeing more red wines on our shelves, as more of the country's vineyard area (40 per cent) is given over to black grapes, notably Pinot Noir.

Germany at a glance

Eighth largest producing nation; world-class Riesling; highly complex classification and labelling.

Mosel – Including Saar and Ruwer, this region is the source of the lightest and most delicate of German Rieslings. Due to their high acidity, the best of these wines have some sweetness to balance this.

Rheingau – Sweet or dry, austere and mineral, elegant wines. Riesling is grown on all the best sites.

Nahe/Rheinhessen – Many softer, off-dry (halbtrocken) wines and a range of grape varieties.

Pfalz – Sunny, warm region where the Rieslings are full, ripe and often grapefruit-scented, and higher in alcohol than those from further north. Increasingly popular for reds, such as Dornfelder and Pinot Noir (called Spätburgunder here).

Baden – Source of much of Germany's Pinot Noir, plus good Pinot Gris (Grauburgunder) and Pinot Blanc (Weissburgunder).

Franken – Distinctive dumpy bottles; good area for white wine from the Silvaner grape.

If you buy German wine, you can expect clean, crisp flavours, usually unmasked by oak. Although many of the wines are now quite dry and therefore higher in alcohol (because a greater proportion of the grape sugar is fermented to alcohol), Germany's moderate climate ensures that its wines are never heavy or overripe.

Germany is the undisputed source of the world's finest wines made from Riesling, the country's most-planted grape. Historically, the best German wines have always been sweet Rieslings. These have little in common with the cheap and fairly sickly supermarket wines that gave German wine a bad name. They are delicate, fragrant and fruity wines, light in body and alcohol and ranging in sweetness from off-dry to richly sweet. The appeal of these wines lies in their fine balance between grapey sweetness and crisp, refreshing acidity, a balance that reflects perfectly the cool growing conditions that prevail in Germany. Their low alcohol (typically between eight per cent and ten per cent) is another refreshing point of difference. They can be enjoyed young, or can live and evolve for decades.

Try these

Must-try German wines:

- Riesling, Riesling, Riesling – it's still what Germany does best. German labels are confusing, but here are a few pointers for quality. Look for the letters QmP (which stands for Qualitätswein mit Prädikat) and the ripeness classification (see terms below), which gives an indication of sweetness. This may be followed by the word 'trocken', in which case the wine will be dry (for more detailed information on German wine labels, see Chapter 12)
- Kabinett – guaranteed light, fresh and low in alcohol, sweet but never cloying
- Spätlese – sweeter, but still usually pretty light
- Auslese – getting quite sweet and rich, sometimes very sweet
- Beerenauslese – very sweet, often made with berries affected by noble rot
- Trockenbeerenauslese – rare and expensive, very intense and sweet
- Eiswein – hard to find and even more expensive, made from grapes left on the vine to freeze.

Portugal

For such an important wine-producing country, Portugal remains peculiarly unknown to most of us. Yet its wines are eminently worthy of discovery. While the rest of the world has largely followed the populist but unoriginal trend towards familiar international varieties, Portugal continues to be loyal to the native grapes from which most of its wines are still made. Unfortunately for Portugese producers, their reluctance to

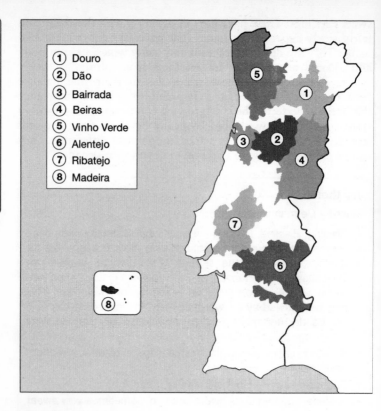

figure 8.5 wine regions of Portugal

conform to the usual mould means that they have to work extra hard to convince everyone to drink their out-of-the-ordinary offerings, so the selection of wines available can be limited. Gradually, this situation does seem to be improving. These days, some producers are blending their indigenous varieties with more familiar international names, but the wines are still distinctively Portugese. If you ever begin to tire of tasting the same old grape varieties, Portugese wines can provide originality in abundance.

The country is probably best known for its fortified wines, the ports that are made in the northern Douro Valley area, to the east of the town of Oporto. Vines clinging to the hot, rocky slopes here produce concentrated grapes, with firm tannins and acidity. Port is made in a range of styles (including white port and even pink port), but all are sweet and high in alcohol (20 per cent) from the fortification process that arrests alcoholic fermentation. The lighter styles can be enjoyed chilled as aperitifs, over ice or with desserts or cheese; the stronger and more tannic, vintage styles are classic, age-worthy sipping wines that can mature for decades in bottle.

The non-fortified wines of Portugal are a far cry from its hefty ports. Although the same grape varieties are often used, Portuguese table wines are mostly light to medium in body and alcohol, and most are characterized by their fresh acidity and brisk tannins.

Try these

Must-try Portugese wines:

- Vinho Verde – crisp, light, dry, refreshing white
- Douro red – Portugal's best, with big flavours and structure
- Alentejo red – soft and juicy, early-drinking styles
- Aged tawny port – serve chilled to appreciate this nutty, lighter port style.

Europe: beyond the top ten

Beyond the higher volume producers of Europe, there are plenty of gems to look out for from other countries.

Austria

Austria produces wines that are not cheap, but are of impressively high and consistent quality. The whites are most interesting, especially those made from the indigenous Grüner Veltliner grape, which accounts for almost one in three of the country's vines. These wines are dry but not austere, with white pepper spice, yeast, apple and almond flavours. If you can find them, Austrian Rieslings are as deliciously fruity as Germany's, with a broader feel in the mouth, a little more alcohol and slightly softer levels of acidity.

Greece

Greece has a lot more to offer these days than pine-scented, holiday retsina. Look out for sturdy reds with unpronounceable names (though it is useful to remember that Agiorgitiko is more easily recalled as its English translation, St George). The individual and tasty range of dry whites is led by delicious Assyrtiko – definitely worth a try. Greek wines are good to drink with food, as they have lovely fresh acidity and only moderate levels of alcohol.

Eastern Europe

Eastern Europe has pockets of interest. **Romania, Bulgaria** and **Hungary** produce good-value wines from international varieties. **Bulgaria** is making some interesting red wines from Bordeaux varieties, although many are rather lavish in their use of oak. **Hungary** produces commendable reds and whites, but its most famous vinous export is its sweet wine, Tokaj, an epic, aged wine made by a complex process involving nobly-rotted grapes to produce a super-crisp sweet wine with heavy botrytis influence.

England

Long the poor relation in European winemaking, England deserves a mention for its fine sparkling wine production. As the climate of northern Europe warms, England looks increasingly interesting (even to French producers in search of new land) for the production of sparkling wine to rival Champagne in quality. The handful of top producers looks set to grow.

09

wine regions: the new world

In this chapter you will learn:
- which styles of wine are made in the different new world countries
- which wines to choose from each country.

It's clear why wines from the new world have met with such success. For the most part, they are packed with sunny, ripe fruit and can be enjoyed practically as soon as the flavours are captured in a bottle. These are wines that are made with the pleasure of the drinker in mind – a curious but real distinction between the new world and some of the more inwardly-focused old world regions. Most of the wines describe on the front label exactly what is in the bottle, in plain English. It's a refreshing change from the bewildering array of classifications and subclassifications of European wines, where grape varieties are often mentioned only as an afterthought and the onus is on you to try to work out what is likely to be in the bottle you buy. Is it any wonder we love wines from the new world?

United States

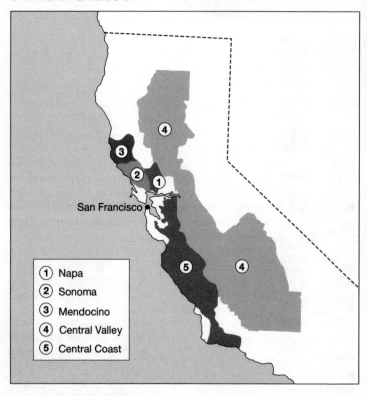

figure 9.1 wine regions of California

USA at a glance

Fourth largest producer; 188 American Viticultural Areas (AVAs – though don't expect to find this term on a wine label).

California – *The* key production area, with both established and up-and-coming regions. Renowned for Cabernet from the small area of Napa Valley, but a vast range of quality and styles elsewhere make up the bulk of the country's production; many grape varieties grown. The largest producing region is the Central Valley, to the south of San Francisco. Most wine labelled 'California' will come from grapes grown here. Historically of fairly basic quality, there are now some interesting wines being produced here as well. The Central Coast region is cooler and generally of higher quality. Regions to look out for for quality wine include: Sonoma, Carneros, Mendocino, Russian River Valley, Dry Creek Valley, Santa Cruz, Anderson Valley, Alexander Valley.

Oregon – Cooler region, producing some of the country's best Pinot Noir.

Washington – Evolving region, formerly best known for its Merlot and Bordeaux blends, but now showing promise for Riesling and Syrah.

New York – Look out for top quality, crisp, Germanic-style Rieslings from the Finger Lakes area.

It's a matter of debate whether Mark Twain actually did say that the coldest winter he ever spent was a summer in San Francisco – but the remark tells us a lot about the success of American wine, 90 per cent of which comes from vineyards to the north and south of the city. From its latitude, which is on a par with the distinctly warmer climes of southern Europe, the only new world winegrowing region of the northern hemisphere looks like it should be a lot warmer than it actually is. The reason for the cooler-than-expected-climate is the cold Humboldt current of the Pacific Ocean. This is responsible for the daily fogs that roll in from the west through gaps in the hills, reducing temperatures dramatically. This is an effect that is especially pronounced on low-lying land, closer to the coast, and it is this variation in temperature that makes high-quality wine production possible.

Californian wines are full of generous, opulent fruit and, like the wines of Australia, their quality is relatively consistent from one year to the next. The wines are characterized by their sweet fruit profile. Due to the high value placed on fruit ripeness here, and the ease with which it is attained, these are wines that are relatively low in acidity and that can be easily drunk with or without food. The downside is that they can sometimes taste overripe and high in alcohol, especially to European tastes (although there are signs that the fashion for super-ripe wines is diminishing).

At the cheaper end, California offers simple, sweet and unchallenging everyday wines in all colours that are hugely popular, although this segment of the market does little justice to the wide spectrum of choice in California. Unfortunately, good Californian wine comes at a price – and sometimes, a very high one. At the top end you will probably struggle to afford, or even find, the best wines. However, it is still worth moving beyond the basic wines in favour of a little more diversity if you want to enjoy more of what California has to offer. The better wines are full of character and concentrated fruit. They balance the naturally exuberant ripeness of California with structure, acidity and individual flair.

The name most people associate with wine in California is the Napa Valley, north of San Francisco, which is the home of America's finest wines from Cabernet Sauvignon. Despite its fame, Napa produces only four per cent of California's grapes. It is further divided into sub-regions according to the soils. Travelling north up the valley, the climate gets warmer and the wines progressively richer. Key sub-regions to look for when buying Cabernet within Napa include Rutherford, Oakville and Stags Leap.

Outside California, there are some wonderful, if hard to find, wines from Oregon, Washington and New York state, especially from cooler climate varieties such as Pinot Noir and Riesling.

Zinfandel – the grape of California

Known as California's own grape (although it actually originates in Croatia), Zinfandel is certainly the grape California has made its own and of which Californians are justly proud – so much so that they even hold an annual festival in honour of the grape. 'Zin' is an unusual black grape that ripens unevenly, so you can find unripe grapes and shrivelled, raisined grapes within the same bunch. The wines are usually sweetly fruity (though rarely actually sweet) and quite soft, often with a raisined character. They are typically pretty alcoholic (it's not uncommon to find Zinfandel at over 15 per cent alcohol). Hugely appreciated in the United States,

Zinfandel is less well known elsewhere, but certainly worth seeking out. The styles range from simple, sugary, light-bodied rosés (much lower in alcohol and labelled 'white Zinfandel') to deeply-coloured, full-blown monster wines.

Where to go in the USA to find the wines you like

- **Cabernet Sauvignon** – California's most planted grape is found everywhere, but is especially good from Napa Valley. Sonoma wines are also a good bet, especially Alexander Valley. For a cooler climate style, try Washington State.
- **Merlot** – Sonoma, Washington.
- **Pinot Noir** – Oregon, Russian River Valley (especially Green Valley), Carneros, Santa Barbara's Santa Rita Hills, Anderson Valley.
- **Zinfandel** – Sonoma (especially Dry Creek Valley), Paso Robles, Mendocino.
- **Syrah/Shiraz** – Washington, Edna Valley, Sonoma, Carneros, Paso Robles.
- **Chardonnay** – Grown everywhere, but try Sonoma, Oregon, Washington, Carneros, Russian River Valley.
- **Riesling** – Washington State, Finger Lakes (New York), Anderson Valley.
- **Gewurztraminer/Viognier** – Little grown, but try Anderson Valley, Mendocino.
- **Sauvignon Blanc** – Grown everywhere, oaked styles (often called Fumé Blanc) from Napa and Sonoma.
- **Sparkling wines** – Carneros, Anderson Valley.

Try these

A taste of California – steer clear of the cheap brands to find more flavour and interest in these wines:

- Chardonnay – pick any region and Chardonnay will be there; the styles range from the buttery, peachy, vanilla-oaked examples to lighter, more lemony wines with less obvious oak
- Cabernet Sauvignon – expect intense, berry fruit and soft tannins in most of the wines
- Zinfandel – pick a deeply coloured example to get an idea of this rich, fruity grape's style
- Sauvignon Blanc – less piercing acidity, sweeter fruit, more tropical in style than other new world countries.

Australia

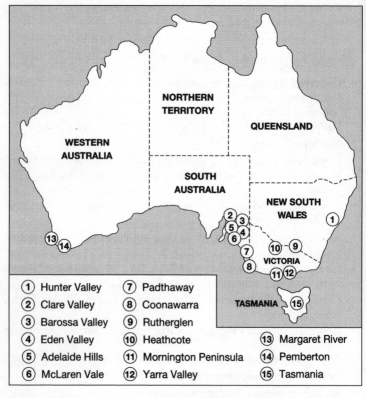

figure 9.2 wine regions in Australia

Australia has been so wildly successful as a wine-growing nation, and in such a short period, that it's hard to imagine life without a plentiful supply of Aussie bottled sunshine to hand. But this looks set to change. There was a time when it looked as though nothing could stop Australia's confident assault on the traditional wines of the old world. If today's climate predictions are correct, though, the combination of heat and (especially) drought may make Australia increasingly unviable as a source of cheap, cheerful wine. High volume, irrigated vineyards are likely to be replaced by smaller, niche producers, and specific regions of production will become far more important than they have been until now.

Australia at a glance

Sixth largest producer; more than 100 Geographical Indications (GIs).

South Eastern Australia – Catch-all Geographical Indication (GI) that includes over 90 per cent of Australia's vineyard area (so wines from here can be from most almost anywhere). Easy-going, unchallenging blends for the most part.

South Australia – The heart of the Australian wine industry. Vineyards around Adelaide produce much of the country's trademark wine, Shiraz. Cooler sites are renowned for Riesling (in particular) and Chardonnay. The key regions of South Australia are Barossa Valley, McLaren Vale, Eden Valley, Clare Valley, Adelaide Hills and, further south, Coonawarra and Padthaway. The latter two regions are best known for Cabernet-based wines.

Victoria – A range of growing conditions means that Victoria produces many varied styles of wine, from the 'stickies' of the hot north to elegant Pinot Noirs in the coastal south. Key regions to look for are Yarra Valley and Mornington Peninsula (both cooler climates), Rutherglen and Heathcote.

New South Wales – Many basic-level vineyards from the vast inland irrigation region of Riverina, plus distinctive, cool climate-style, early-picked Semillon and Shiraz wines from the definitely-not-cool Hunter Valley, north of Sydney.

Western Australia – Top-quality wines from the cooler areas south of Perth. Look out for Margaret River, Pemberton and Mount Barker.

Tasmania – Australia's chilliest state, most noted for its high-quality sparkling wine production.

Australian wine styles: a question of climate

If you buy Australian wine you are buying ripeness and clean, fresh styles. Contrary to what you may have experienced with some so-called 'traditional' European wines, you are unlikely to find unpleasant or unfamiliar smells wafting from a glass of wine from Down Under. You're also less likely to find the wine tainted by problems associated with the cork, since so many of the producers have switched to using screwcaps to keep their wines as fresh as the day they were bottled (see Chapter 13 for more about this).

The flavours you expect from the various different grape varieties (see Chapter 03) will be pretty faithfully rendered in Australian wines. Beyond this, the key to understanding the different styles of wine is to look at the region they come from. Australia's huge land mass has a vast range of climates and soil types. But in spite of these stylistic differences, if a wine is from Australia you can, in most cases, expect it to be bigger, riper and higher in alcohol than an equivalent wine from Europe.

Where to go in Australia to find the wines you like

- **Shiraz** – Grown in most places, but especially Barossa Valley and McLaren Vale
- **Cabernet Sauvignon** – Coonawarra, Padthaway, Margaret River
- **Merlot** – Adelaide Hills
- **Pinot Noir** – Mornington Peninsula, Yarra Valley
- **Grenache** – Barossa Valley
- **Riesling** – Clare Valley, Eden Valley
- **Chardonnay** – Yarra Valley, Tasmania, Adelaide Hills, Margaret River, Mornington Peninsula
- **Sémillon** – Everywhere, but especially Hunter Valley and Margaret River
- **Sauvignon Blanc** – Adelaide Hills
- **Sparkling wines** – Tasmania, Yarra Valley
- **Sweet, fortified** – Rutherglen
- **Milder flavours** – South Eastern Australia.

Try these

For big, bold flavours, try this classic Australian tasting:

- Grenache/Shiraz/Mourvèdre from Barossa Valley – masses of chunky, sweet black, spicy fruit, oaky flavours and high alcohol are the hallmarks of the 'GSM' blend
- Cabernet Sauvignon from Coonawarra – plenty of sweet, cassis fruit, some mintiness, firm, dusty tannins and good balance can be expected from this excellent Cabernet region
- Pinot Noir from Yarra Valley – you'll find the fruit more obviously fleshy and riper than it is in Burgundian wines, probably more in the strawberry spectrum of flavours than savoury or mineral; if you like Pinot Noir without too much harsh acidity, Australia is a good place to go

Think all Shiraz tastes the same? Think again. Try this comparative tasting:

- Sparkling Shiraz – an Australian original, this has proper Shiraz flavours, but is soft, juicy, and usually slightly sweet
- Shiraz from Hunter Valley – more European in style, with leathery fruit character and lighter body
- Shiraz from Barossa Valley – classically powerful and intense, with rich, black fruit flavours and spice
- Shiraz from McLaren Vale – in a similar mould to the Barossa style, this neighbouring region produces wines with a sweet, ripe, chocolatey fruit character
- Western Australia – spicy, intense, peppery Shiraz; less immediate than Barossa/McLaren Vale, but can be very good.

For more unusual Australian wines, try these:

- Sémillon from Hunter Valley – hard to believe a region so hot could produce such a feather-light, lemony, low-alcohol style as this. The secret? They pick the grapes really early to retain their freshness
- Riesling from Clare Valley – the antithesis of big, oaky Chardonnay, this is an invigorating, lime-scented Australian classic; the best Riesling in the new world
- Liqueur Muscat from Rutherglen – amazingly sweet, treacly, nutty wine that has to be tasted to be believed.

Chile

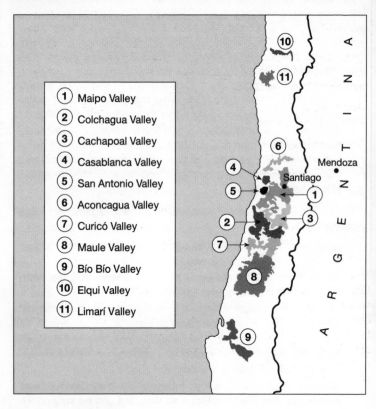

1. Maipo Valley
2. Colchagua Valley
3. Cachapoal Valley
4. Casablanca Valley
5. San Antonio Valley
6. Aconcagua Valley
7. Curicó Valley
8. Maule Valley
9. Bío Bío Valley
10. Elqui Valley
11. Limarí Valley

figure 9.3 wine regions in Chile

Chile at a glance

Eleventh largest producer; Denominations of Origin (DO) for four main regions and 13 sub-regions.

Maipo Valley – Historic vineyard area, close to the capital, Santiago. Best known for structured, sometimes minty wines from Cabernet Sauvignon, and Bordeaux blends.

Colchagua Valley/Cachapoal Valley – Warmer regions south of Santiago. Riper, juicier, often simpler styles of Cabernet Sauvignon compared with Maipo, and particularly successful reds from Merlot and Carmenère.

Casablanca Valley/ San Antonio Valley – Cool-climate regions close to the coast, west of Santiago. Casablanca is more established, but the cooler San Antonio Valley is generating much excitement for quality wines. Very good Sauvignon Blanc (especially from Leyda sub-region), good Chardonnay and the best Pinot Noir in the country. Also some interesting Syrah is emerging from Casablanca.

Aconcagua Valley – Small, warm region north of Santiago. Produces full-bodied wines from a range of varieties.

Curicó Valley/Maule Valley – Large regions producing correct, if rarely spectacular, wines from all the usual suspects: Cabernet Sauvignon, Sauvignon Blanc, Chardonnay and Carmenère.

Bío Bío Valley – Southern region with a cold climate, producing small quantities of good Pinot Noir and aromatic white wines.

Elqui Valley/Limarí Valley – Northern regions making some of Chile's most exciting new wine styles, especially Syrah blends and Sauvignon Blanc.

Chile has quickly established itself as a producer of well-priced wines the world wants to drink. Average quality is now very consistent for the country's key calling cards of Cabernet Sauvignon and Sauvignon Blanc. As new wine-growing regions are discovered, and curious winemakers explore the possibilities of their terrain, Chile becomes an ever more interesting source of quality wine.

North to south, or east to west? Do Chile's regions matter?

Even from looking at a map, you can see that Chile's geography is nothing short of dramatic: a 4,000 kilometre-long sliver of a country dominated by the Andes mountains, clinging to the edge of the South American continent. The country's unusual topography has a clear impact on its wines.

Chilean wine regions are broadly divided north to south. The region you will probably see most often on a bottle is the Central Valley, which (rather like the Geographical Indication of South Eastern Australia) is the one that means the least, incorporating as it does most of Chile's vines (more than 80 per cent at last count). The Central Valley comprises the more meaningful sub-zones of Maipo, Colchagua, Cachapoal, Curicó and Maule. The wide valleys of the country's centre produce the predictable, fruity and generally inexpensive reds for which Chile is appreciated.

Although it seems the most obvious way to look at Chile, north-to-south is less relevant for most regions than east-to-west. Away from the warmer, flatter land of the centre, the climate and conditions for growing grapes can alter over remarkably short distances (which is just as well, since all distances from east to west are quite short in Chile). To the east, it is the mountains that make the difference. Here, grapes are cooled (especially at night) by mountain breezes, which counter the heat of the day and give wines more freshness and a greater range of flavours. To the west, it is the cold air from the Pacific Ocean that is a constant presence in the vineyards. This favours the production of varieties that only give of their best in a cool climate, such as Pinot Noir, Sauvignon Blanc and Chardonnay.

Chile's own grape

It's worth looking out for Carmenère, the Bordeaux grape Chile has claimed as its own. Not quite as ubiquitous as Shiraz in Australia, or Malbec in Argentina, this is the grape that people used to think was Merlot. (If you were drinking Chilean wine labelled 'Merlot' ten years ago, the chances are it was Carmenère.) These days, Carmenère is being sold for what it is. Much of it is really very good – and usually a lot more interesting than Merlot. It has the black fruit character and supple tannins of Merlot, but added spicy, tobacco dimensions too. This is a grape that ripens late, so choose a Carmenère wine from a warm region like Colchagua to avoid any green, unripe flavours.

Try these

Chilean wine is reliably good at lower prices. Try the simple, frank flavours of Cabernet Sauvignon, Carmenère, Chardonnay and Sauvignon Blanc. If you like those, see how much more you can get for your money if you move on to these:

- Sauvignon Blanc from Leyda – this is as good as it gets in Chile; the Sauvignons from the coast here have a dry, grassy, mineral intensity that recalls a gentler version of New Zealand's powerful flavours

- Syrah from Elqui Valley or Limarí Valley – these far-north regions seem to have a magical effect on Syrah, producing wines of great purity and delicious fruit character; they have the sweet fruit of Australia but less of the body – hence the decision to label the wine Syrah, to orient it more towards the French model of the grape
- Cabernet Sauvignon blend from Maipo Valley – the original quality wine from Chile can still hold its own against more fashionable, newer regions
- Carmenère blend from Colchagua – satisfying, richly flavoured wine.

Argentina

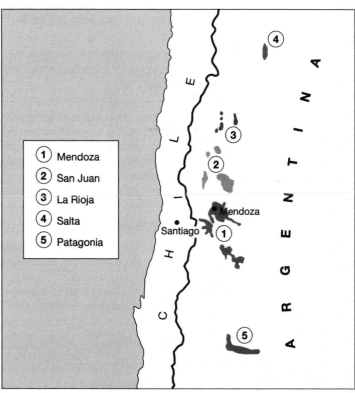

1. Mendoza
2. San Juan
3. La Rioja
4. Salta
5. Patagonia

figure 9.4 wine regions in Argentina

Argentina at a glance

Fifth largest producer.

Mendoza – By far the most important wine-producing region for both quality and quantity, close to the city of Mendoza. Reds predominate. Malbec and Cabernet Sauvignon are everywhere, but many other grapes, often of Italian and Spanish origin, are also grown, including Bonarda, Tempranillo, Barbera and Petit Verdot. Quality sub-regions to look out for within Mendoza include Luján de Cuyo, Tupungato and Valle de Uco. Altitude is important here: the better vineyards are higher up to benefit from cool night-time temperatures.

San Juan and La Rioja – Warmer regions north of Mendoza. Some very good Syrah/Shiraz coming from San Juan.

Salta – Northern, high-altitude vineyards producing some remarkable wines. Best known for fragrant, full-bodied Torrontès whites.

Patagonia – Cool, fruit-growing region with difficult growing conditions. Some promising new vineyards for lighter styles of Malbec, Merlot, Chardonnay and Pinot Noir.

Argentina has long been a major wine producer and drinker of its own wines, but it is only recently that it has become a serious wine-exporting nation. After a slow start, and trailing in the wake of its dynamic neighbour, Chile, Argentina is now starting to produce some really exciting wines from a wide range of grape varieties that offer big flavours and great value for money.

Malbec, Malbec and yet more Malbec

If you've tasted Argentinian wine recently, it was probably made from Malbec grapes. Argentina may have the most interesting mix of grape varieties anywhere, yet it is for Malbec that it is known, often to the exclusion of all else. This is a bit of a shame, since Argentina has as diverse a range of grape varieties as you'll find anywhere.

Argentina does make good Malbec, though. The wines, deeply coloured and aromatic, usually look a lot more challenging than they taste. Malbec is easy to enjoy, as it is full of juicy, sweet, black cherry and blackcurrant fruit but has quite a soft structure. If you enjoy the lush flavours of Malbec, try a wine made from a blend of Malbec and Cabernet to taste the difference.

Beyond Malbec, there are interesting reds to try from Syrah/Shiraz (both names are used here), Barbera, Tempranillo and Bonarda. Whites are currently less of a focus in Argentina, but the local Torrontès grape makes a unique and highly aromatic wine reminiscent of Gewurztraminer or Muscat. Chardonnay is better than you might expect, though there is unfortunately little interest in making it.

Try these

Top tips for Argentina – don't miss out on these:

- Malbec – try wines from different regions to taste the difference
- Malbec blends – arguably offering a more interesting range of flavours than the single variety, these can be delicious
- Barbera – crisp, but more approachable than its Italian equivalent
- Syrah – search for one from San Juan, where growing conditions seem naturally suited to this grape
- Cabernet Sauvignon – ripe, but rarely overripe, this is a grape than can produce really good results in Argentina
- Torrontès from Salta – uniquely Argentinian, fragrant, sweet-smelling (but usually dry) white.

South Africa

South Africa at a glance

Ninth largest producer. Regionality expressed as Wine of Origin on the label.

Stellenbosch – The most important region in South Africa.

Paarl and Franschoek – Warmer neighbouring regions, inland from Stellenbosch.

Constantia – Historic region close to Cape Town, producing good Sauvignon Blanc and a small quantity of sweet Vin de Constance.

Walker Bay – Look out for cool-climate wines from this coastal region south-east of Cape Town.

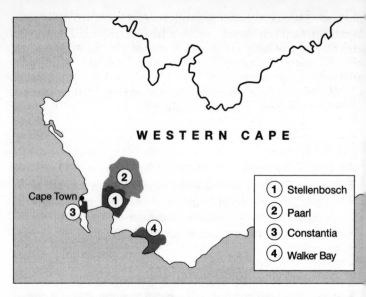

figure 9.5 wine regions in South Africa

Of all the new world countries, South Africa is the one most readily compared to the old world. This is partly because of its long history of winegrowing from European settlers, but mostly for the styles of wine it produces. In spite of its long history, South Africa is a country very much still in transition today and offers many opportunities for vinous discovery, at competitive prices.

The best wines of South Africa bridge the ripeness of the new world with the tight structure of the old world to create distinctive wines of elegance and longevity. In common with several of the world's regions where one would expect the climate to be hot, South Africa's viticulture is made possible by a cold ocean influence, this time the Benguela current from the Antarctic. This mitigates the heat of the African sun.

South African whites

Around 55 per cent of South African wine is white, but the balance has been shifting swiftly towards red wine in recent years, mostly at the expense of the country's most-planted variety, Chenin Blanc. South African white wines frequently have crisp acidity that recalls cooler, European regions of origin.

Chenin Blanc and Colombard (the second most-planted white grape) can be both tart and bland (or light and refreshing, depending on your point of view). However, there are some worthy wines from Chenin Blanc to be found in South Africa, made from the produce of older vines (and there are more old vines from Chenin than anything else). Blends (with Viognier or Chardonnay, for example) are also worth trying for an interesting array of flavours.

South African Sauvignon Blanc has generated considerable interest in recent years, and with good reason. These wines offer the cool, crisp, grassy character that typifies Sauvignon from France's Loire Valley, combined with a broader, fuller weight of fruit in the mouth. It is a winning and unique combination.

Chardonnay has suffered the same declining popularity in South Africa as elsewhere, but there are some delicious and elegant wines produced from the variety here, especially from cooler sites such as Elgin and Walker Bay.

South African reds: beyond Pinotage

Red wines from South Africa are distinctive, from a combination of growing conditions and grape varieties. South Africa's own grape variety is Pinotage, which is made as a single varietal wine or blended. While it may be South Africa's best-known grape variety, few these days consider it to represent the best the country can do. It produces wines in various styles, from light and fruity to deeply coloured, oak-aged examples. The flavours of Pinotage are somewhat curious; the wines are certainly fruity and pungent, and some people love its intensity. But it is often also accompanied by whiffs of things you might not want to drink: bananas, paint, or rubber, for example. It's one of those things you just have to try for yourself (and I should add that some are quite delicious!).

While Pinotage has fallen from favour slightly, Cabernet Sauvignon and Syrah have been the main beneficiaries of the new vine plantings. As with the whites, these wines usually have good levels of acidity. The fruit, while ripe, never seems to attain the super-ripe character that one finds in other countries of the new world, which leads to comparisons with European wines. Moreover, South Africa is proving a popular place for new investments from Bordeaux, so expect to see an increase in the number of French-styled wines coming out of the country.

You may notice that red wines from South Africa are often characterized by burnt rubber or green, 'leafy' aromas. Some people find this character perfectly acceptable, and part of the appeal of South African wines, while others dislike it. The source of these aromas is not well understood and is under investigation, although in some cases it is thought to be linked to the health of the vines.

Try these

Must-try South African wines:

- Sauvignon Blanc – grassy, fresh, delicious
- Chenin Blanc – for the most part, light and easy-drinking styles
- Chardonnay – you may be surprised at just how unlike a new world Chardonnay these wines are
- Pinotage – the classic South African grape
- Syrah/Shiraz – spicy and rich, modern in style
- Cabernet blends – the best are stylish and ripe, with intriguing new world/old world character.

New Zealand

Small but significant, New Zealand's main contribution to wine is its unmistakably pungent Sauvignon Blanc, which sells faster than the Kiwis can grow it. But New Zealand has plenty of other delicious wines up its sleeve. Most aromatic white grapes grow well here and the country is also making a name for itself with super-stylish, succulent Pinot Noirs that are the best examples of this grape variety in the new world (and some might say, anywhere).

New Zealand produces some of the most consistently high-quality wines in the world, a fact that is reflected in their above-average prices. New Zealand just doesn't do plonk. The wines are remarkable for their pure, concentrated fruit flavours, unfailing freshness and aromatic intensity, a combination that few other places in the world can match.

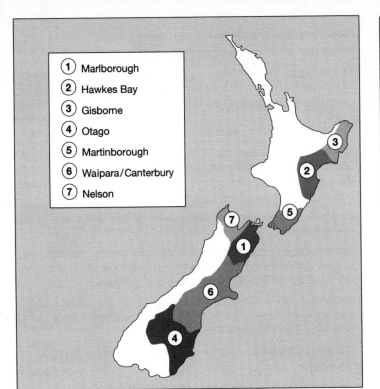

1. Marlborough
2. Hawkes Bay
3. Gisborne
4. Otago
5. Martinborough
6. Waipara/Canterbury
7. Nelson

figure 9.6 wine regions in New Zealand

New Zealand's greatest strengths lie in its aromatic white wines and Pinot Noir. Sauvignon Blanc is the country's most successful export. The dramatically full-on, grassy style epitomized by the Sauvignons of Marlborough is now even copied by the French. But the greatest excitement these days is reserved for New Zealand's Pinot Noirs, especially those from the young vines planted in Central Otago. These wines are probably the most sensuously scented examples of this grape to be found anywhere. There are some interesting Pinot Gris wines to seek out, typically in a heavy, silky-textured style. Chardonnay is unfashionable and underrated, but can be very good in New Zealand, especially from the Hawkes Bay area.

New Zealand at a glance

Young and dynamic wine-producing nation.

Marlborough – Home of the most distinctive New Zealand Sauvignon Blanc and the majority of the country's vineyards. Most of the land is given over to Sauvignon Blanc, but there are also smaller quantities of Pinot Noir, Chardonnay and aromatic whites such as Riesling and Pinot Gris. Significant quantities of sparkling wine are produced here.

Hawkes Bay – Known for its full-flavoured Chardonnays and red wines from Bordeaux grapes, Merlot and Cabernet, the growers of this sunny region are now also turning their attention to Syrah, with promising results.

Gisborne – Produces soft and peachy Chardonnays and good aromatic whites.

Central Otago – Young wine region, the most southerly in the world, producing attention-grabbing Pinot Noirs. Aromatic white wines are also of note, from Riesling and Pinot Gris in particular.

Martinborough – Situated at the south of the North Island, Martinborough's reputation is for its fine, densely fruited Pinot Noirs. Chardonnay and Sauvignon Blanc are also good.

Waipara/Canterbury – Another good and potentially great region for Pinot Noir.

Nelson – Notable for Chardonnay and Pinot Noir.

Try these

- Sauvignon Blanc from Marlborough – the Kiwi classic
- Pinot Noir from Central Otago – this is floral, scented and practically jumping out of the glass, with silky, red-fruit flavours and warm alcohol
- Pinot Noir from Martinborough – still highly aromatic, but with denser, black fruit and greater concentration compared to the fruit of the younger vines of Central Otago.

The rest of the new world

Unless you have travelled to **China**, you have probably never seen, let alone tasted, a Chinese wine. Although China is the world's sixth largest producer of wine, little of the wine leaves the country and the quality is unexciting. The young wine industry is growing rapidly, however, and it is likely that the best spots for viticulture have yet to be found. **Uruguay** is known for its wines from the Tannat grape, which produces more consistent results here than it does in France. The wines are firm and full-flavoured and gaining recognition for their quality.

part four

buying, serving and storing wine

10

wine with food

In this chapter you will learn:
- how to drink the wine you want with the food you want
- how to avoid food and wine clashes
- what to do if the wine you've chosen *doesn't* taste good with your food.

It's one of the most talked about and mystifying of subjects: the art of matching wine with food. If this is a subject that impassions you, there is an entire industry of books dedicated to what goes with what – or not. But how much advice on food and wine matching is really useful, or even accurate? With an infinite number of flavour combinations and cuisines, and with wines changing from one vintage to the next, it is virtually impossible to find exactly the right wine match for every dish in every situation. We are led to believe that red wine is the 'correct' thing to drink with steak and that fish is best served with white wine. But what are these rules based on? And what happens if you break them?

What follows is an alternative way of looking at food and wine, one that doesn't require years of experimentation or constant references to lists of food and wine pairings, and one that doesn't require you to drink wines you may not like, just for the sake of creating the 'right' combination to enjoy with a certain dish. How much more enjoyable would it be to drink the wine you like with any food you want to eat? Believe it or not, it can be done. This chapter could change the way you think about food and wine forever.

Here's something to think about: how often have you actually been disappointed by how your wine matches your food? My guess is that the answer is seldom or never. What you are more likely to remember is whether you disliked the wine you drank with your dinner. This may be related to the fact that it did not match the food. Or it may not. It may be that you didn't like the wine in the first place and the food did not change that impression.

A new way of thinking about wine and food is to start with the wine you want to drink. If you have read the previous chapters you will by now be in a good position to do this, and to understand why you like the wines you like. Your preferences will be based on the wines' structure and flavours. The next step is to look at how the wines taste when you drink them with food.

Undoubtedly, you will have been drinking wine with food, but now you need to pay particular attention to the structure of your wine and to see how this changes when you eat different foods. This approach dispenses, at least in the first instance, with thinking about flavours. This comes later and is quite straightforward, once the structure is in place. You will see that focusing on matching the structure of wine and food is a simple and effective way of matching any wine with any food – thereby enabling you to drink the wine you like, every time.

The five basic taste sensations

The human palate can detect a very limited number of tastes. So far, these have been identified as:

* sweet
* sour
* bitter
* salty
* umami.

The first four of these are familiar tastes to most people. The fifth, umami, has only gained widespread recognition since the 1980s.

Check your taste – and explode the myth of the 'tongue map'

Have you ever checked whether the 'tongue map' – still taught in schools today – actually works? Conventional wisdom has it that various areas of the tongue taste differently: we taste sweetness at the tip of the tongue, salt in the middle, bitterness at the back and acidity (sourness) at the sides. While it is true that our tongues may be more sensitive in some areas than others to these different tastes, if you test these flavours you will find you can taste them all over your tongue.

Try this

Isolate the five basic tastes and remove the influence of your far more sensitive sense of smell by holding your nose while you taste:

Sweet: sugar
Sour: lemon juice
Bitter: dark, leafy greens or coffee
Salty: salt
Umami: unseasoned beef, cooked mushrooms.

What is umami?

A Japanese scientist, Kikunae Ikeda of Tokyo Imperial University, discovered umami in 1908, although it was subsequently ignored by the world for most of the rest of the century, perhaps because it is less obvious as a taste compared to the other four tastes detectable by our palates. Umami is a Japanese word that has no direct translation but essentially means 'deliciousness'. It is glutamate formed from amino acids that makes food taste savoury and appealing in a way that the other four tastes do not; it is the *raison d'être* of monosodium glutamate, adding savoury completeness to dishes. Umami is present in a wide range of foods in different amounts, notably ripe tomatoes, parmesan cheese, mushrooms, soy and red meats. It accounts for the popularity of Marmite and Maggi sauce. Curing and fermentation raise the levels of umami in food.

Umami came to be accepted as the 'fifth taste' from the 1980s, but it was only in 2002 that two American scientists, Charles S. Zuker and Nicholas J. P. Ryba, proved that the human palate can physically taste the amino acids from which it derives.

Umami in wine

It seems logical that wine will have umami as well as food, since umami is related to ripeness and fermentation flavours and wine does contain amino acids. American Master of Wine, Tim Hanni, specializes in what he calls 'flavour balancing' when matching wine and food and has a particular interest in the effects of umami. He is convinced that wines have umami. So far, nobody has come up with a way of measuring this, or (even better) a list of umami-rich wines. But it does seem that foods high in umami taste have a negative effect on wine, so the umami in the food needs to be countered, or balanced, with other flavours. The theory is that umami in food will diminish umami in wine, thus reducing its deliciousness. Applying these theories opens up a new perspective on enjoying wine with food.

How the five tastes in food affect the flavours of wine

If you understand how to balance the basic tastes in food and wine, it is much easier to create a harmonious match.

The main thing to remember is that a predominance of any one taste in your food will diminish the impact of that taste in the wine you are drinking. This is the reason it is often hard to match a sweet wine with a sweet dessert: the wine needs to be sweeter than the food in order for you to taste its sweetness at all, let alone for it to taste good. Sweet food with dry wine is not a happy combination. The sweetness in the food will accentuate any tannins, acidity or bitterness in the wine.

Very sour food will reduce the perception of acidity in wine, making it appear smoother. Depending on how you like your wine to taste, you might see this as a good thing, or you might want to choose a more acidic wine so that your drinking more closely matches your eating. A food high in umami will have the same effect on a wine as sugar. The fruit will appear diminished and the acidity and tannin will become more prominent.

With red wine, managing the perception of tannins is a bigger challenge than matching specific flavours in your food. Anything that is sweet or spicy will accentuate the astringency of tannins in red wine. Salty and fatty foods work well to smooth out tannins, as does seasoned red meat.

Testing flavour balancing for yourself

The only real way to test this type of flavour balancing is to try it for yourself. For this experiment, you will need:

- cooked beef (steak or mince), unseasoned
- cooked white fish, unseasoned
- cooked mushrooms, unseasoned
- a piece of hard cheese (such as Cheddar or Parmesan)
- a glass of red wine you like
- a glass of white wine you like
- a lemon
- salt.

1 Taste the wines and write yourself a tasting note for each, paying particular attention to the structure of the wines and how they feel in your mouth. Note the nature of the fruit profile of the wines, whether or not you feel the wines to be in balance, and how much you like each one.

2 Taste the white wine again, then eat a small piece of the fish and taste the white wine again. Note any changes you perceive in the wine. Do you like it more or less than before? Repeat this with the red wine. Which tasted better with the food, the red or the white?

3 Taste the white wine again, to remind you of the original taste. Now take a piece of fish and add a little salt and a good squeeze of lemon juice. Now taste the wine again. Does it taste any different? Note any apparent differences. Repeat with the red wine.

4 Now repeat steps 2 and 3 with the beef, the mushrooms and the cheese.

If you are focusing on the effect of the food on the wine here (rather than the effect of the wine on the food, or whether you like the combination of the two), you will probably find that unseasoned beef, fish and mushrooms have a detrimental effect on the taste of the wine. All will accentuate the tannins in the red wine and reduce the fruitiness of both red and white wines. In short, they will change how the wine tastes. By adding lemon and salt to each food, you will probably find that it tastes better but that, more importantly, the wine tastes more like it did before you had any food. If you go on to taste the wine again, on its own, you will find it starts to taste more like it did when you first tasted it again. What about the cheese? It is one of the greatest food matching myths that red wine and cheese were made for each other. As you may have seen here, cheese accentuates the tannins in red wine. White wine (sweet or dry) is almost always a better choice to drink with cheese.

Assuming the taste of the wine before you started eating is a taste you like and want, the lesson is that something needs to be done to your food to ensure that your wine tastes as you want it to. Now if you find you *don't* like the wine you've bought, it's quite likely the food may make it taste better! A red wine lacking in acidity or tannin may be enlivened by a dish that makes it seem more vibrant and crisp. Or a white wine you may have found a little heavy and creamy could prove perfect when matched with a dish whose richness makes the wine seem less so.

Adding lemon and salt creates the necessary salt and acidity to balance the umami in the food. In most cuisines, acidity and salt would be added in the form of seasoning and sauces – though not necessarily to the right degree for a particular wine (or for your own taste). If you are the cook, check the seasoning of your dish with the wine you plan to drink and try to adjust accordingly. Once you see what happens when you combine different flavours like this, matching food and wine suddenly seems rather simple.

Lemon and salt: can it really be that straightforward?

Surely, there has to be a little more to food and wine matching than keeping a supply of lemon and salt to hand? Well, yes and no. The usual rationale for combining wine with certain foods is one of two things: either choose a wine that complements the flavours in the food, or choose a wine that provides a contrast, that compensates for deficiencies in the food. Certainly, there are some flavours in wine that match beautifully with the flavours in food: buttery Chardonnay with creamy fish; tangy oysters with mineral Chablis; mature Pinot Noir with rich, mushroom-based sauce, and so on. But the important point to matching a wine with a dish is that unless the basic balance of the tastes is right, the wine will probably not taste as good as it should.

The only way wine can truly provide a compensating role to the food is if the two are consumed at exactly the same time. If you try this, you will see that it does work – but it is not how most people choose to eat and drink (at least, not in the company of others). It is far better to get the balance of tastes in the food right first, and then enjoy the wine for the aromas and flavours that harmonize with the food. Paying attention to how the taste of your wine changes with food will enable you to adjust your choices accordingly. And if you would really prefer to drink red wine than white, no matter what you are eating, understanding how to balance the flavours in your food to compensate for the structure of the wine will enable you to enjoy strong, tannic Cabernet Sauvignon with just about anything.

Top tip

If you like the powerful taste of Fino sherry, you're in luck: it's delicious with many foods. Could it be that it is high in umami?

Other things to think about

If you start with your wine preferences, you can usually find a way to make wine work with any food. If you are planning a dinner at home, think about the flavours in your food, and their intensity and weight. Try to be bold with your food and wine ideas, but remember that it will be hard to match a wide range of flavours with just one wine. Generally speaking, choose a lighter wine with lighter food and a more full-bodied wine with bigger flavours. If you are opening a special wine, think less about matching its flavours and more about not overwhelming it with flavours from the food. The finest wines are best served with simple food. Strong soft cheeses, in particular, can obliterate the flavours of a delicate old wine. A few foods are not friendly to wine. These include tomatoes, eggs, chilli, asparagus, artichokes and chocolate. You will need to work harder on the other flavours in your dish to counter the negative effects of these on wine.

serving wine

In this chapter you will learn:
- the best temperature for serving wines
- when to chill red wine
- how and when to decant
- how to choose wine glasses
- the order of serving wines.

There is no right or wrong way to serve wine, particularly in your own home. But there are some useful things to know to make sure you and your guests are likely to enjoy it more.

What is the best temperature for serving wine?

Received wisdom tells us that red wines are served at room temperature and white wines are served chilled. In fact, most wines will taste best somewhere between the two, at a temperature that optimizes the balance in the wine.

Chilling white wine makes it taste more refreshing, but the colder the wine, the less you will appreciate its subtleties of aroma or flavour. Consider how much better tomatoes taste at room temperature (or, best of all, warm and fresh off the plant) compared with when taken straight from the fridge. The colder ones will taste sharper and less sweet and have less flavour. The same will happen with your wine. Chilling a wine will heighten your perception of acidity and diminish its apparent sweetness. It may be preferable for some wines to be served really cold, but as a general rule, the better the wine, the less refrigeration is needed.

When to chill

Most of us prefer white wine served cool, especially in hot weather, when the ambient temperature will quickly warm it in your glass. White wines tend to be drunk within a couple of years of their vintage date, when their vibrant, primary fruit character is to the fore. Wines with bold, youthful appeal but little complexity of aroma or flavour from bottle age, can be served cold with minimal risk of spoiling your enjoyment.

Powerful whites from warm countries, that have plenty of rich flavours but low levels of acidity, can also be served cooler (but remember that any oak will appear more pronounced in a chilled wine). All but the finest rosés will taste crisper and fresher cold. Most sparkling wine is high in acidity, but unless it has especially fine flavours, most people prefer it served quite cold. Unremarkable whites with little flavour can be rendered acceptable, if not exactly thrilling, when chilled.

Refrigeration can be a useful way of adding a perception of crispness to wines made from white grapes with relatively low acidity, such as Muscat, Gewurztraminer or Viognier, although there will be a trade-off in the loss of aromas from these naturally perfumed varieties.

Very sweet and unctuous wines can withstand low temperatures, which will make them taste more refreshing. Don't worry if you see white crystals in the bottom of the bottle when you chill a sweet wine. While you probably won't actually want to swallow them, these are harmless tartrates that precipitate out of the wine on chilling and do not affect its flavour (unlike red wine sediments – see below). They are usually only found in higher quality wines that are made in a more natural way – so if your guests complain, you can tell them that!

Bone-dry Fino sherry styles should always be served cold, and most other sherries benefit from being served from the fridge as well. Sweet sherry is nicely freshened by cooling. Light port styles also suit chilling; tawny and white ports taste far better served cold.

Top tip

To chill several bottles of wine in a hurry put them in a bucket of ice and add water and salt. They will cool much faster than in ice alone.

Chilling red wine

The idea that red wine should be served at a room temperature of between 18°C and 20°C is a recent one, resulting from the rising temperature of our homes; traditionally, wines were always served either straight from the cellar, at a temperature of between 10 and 15°C, or at a cooler room temperature of between 16 and 18°C. Red wines today are often served far too warm.

The most important factor to consider with red wine temperature is how much tannin is in the wine. Chilling will accentuate both tannin and acidity levels, so a heavy Italian or Bordeaux red will taste quite unpleasant when too cold (try it some time and see for yourself just how unpalatable they become). In contrast, soft, light red wines, such as young Beaujolais or Pinot Noir (especially the fruitier, new world styles), light Italian reds such as Valpolicella, or Loire reds will all taste better served lightly chilled. By accentuating the acidity in these wines, the fruit will taste livelier and juicier.

Conversely, for a super-concentrated red wine that is high in alcohol, a light cooling will result in lifted aromatics and a lessening of the perception of burning alcohol. If a wine is too intense, you could even go as far as to add an ice cube to the glass for an immediate burst of aroma and freshness once it is poured (this trick also works for over-alcoholic, concentrated white wines).

> **Top tip**
>
> In hot weather, try chilling your glasses to keep your wine cooler for longer. This is especially good for sparkling wine, but make sure you don't have any strong fridge odours that will linger in the glasses.

When not to chill

Big, tannic red wines (as noted above) will not benefit from being served too cool, as this will accentuate the natural astringency of the tannins to the detriment of the fruit. As a rule, the more tannic the wine, the warmer it should be served.

Beware of over-chilling any fine white wine, regardless of its age. Vintage champagne should be served at a warmer temperature than non-vintage champagne, in order to appreciate the yeasty complexity that will have developed in the bottle.

Serving temperature guideline

Coolest to warmest serving temperatures:

Very cold	Fino sherry
	sparkling wine
	unoaked Spanish whites
	unoaked Italian/French whites
	off-dry non-aromatic whites
	tawny or white port
	rosé
Cold	new world Chardonnay
	Sauvignon Blanc
	other aromatic whites
	oaked whites
	vintage Champagne

Lightly chilled	fine white Burgundy/Chardonnay
	Beaujolais
	new world Pinot Noir
	other light European reds
Cellar temperature	Rioja reds
	red Burgundy
	southern Rhône reds
	new world Shiraz
Room temperature	top Italian reds
	northern Rhône reds
	good Merlot
	fine Cabernet Sauvignon-based wines
	vintage port

Decanting wine: is it necessary?

There are two practical reasons to decant wine. The first is to remove the wine from any deposit in the bottle that might taint its flavour; the second is to aerate the wine.

Decanting is usually associated with fine, old red wines and vintage port, as both will tend to throw a sediment after several years in bottle. Nobody understands exactly what happens to wine as it ages, but we do know that sediment is formed when the tannin structures that bind together in young wine break down and precipitate out of the wine over time. This makes the wine taste softer and more enjoyable, and produces the inimitable flavours and aromas we love in old wine. Once the tannins are in the bottom of the bottle, however, you want them to stay out of your wine, as they will impart bitter flavours if they are concentrated in the bottom of your glass.

Decanting an old wine from its sediment can be a tricky business, requiring a steady hand. Ideally, the wine should be stored upright for a day or so to allow any sediment to gather in the base of the bottle. When you are ready to drink the wine, pour it slowly and steadily into a carafe or decanter, in a good light, so that you can see the deposit and stop pouring at just the right moment. An alternative would be to filter the wine, but as wine ages it becomes more delicate and filtering at this stage would probably strip it of the nuances of flavour that you've been waiting for, or have paid a lot to enjoy.

Most wines you buy will already have been filtered in the winery to remove any unwanted deposit and won't be old enough to have any tannin fall-out. Even wines labelled 'unfiltered' are unlikely to trouble you with unwanted deposits in their first few years of life. But many wines, both red and white, will still taste better if decanted before drinking.

Have you noticed how the last glass in a bottle of wine often tastes better than the first? This is because the wine has been exposed to the air. Decanting wine purely to aerate it can be thought of as a way of speeding up the ageing process. It is particularly beneficial for wines that could benefit from a year or two in bottle before drinking. The oxygen afforded by decanting allows the wine to open up, releasing more of its flavours, more quickly. Tannins become supple and more rounded. A wine that initially seems masked by oak will reveal its fruit. Decanting can also be a great idea for white wines, especially those with some complexity and layers of flavour, which will be brought out with aeration.

There is no need for any special preparation or equipment to decant wine for this reason. There are many beautiful decanters designed to aerate wine in different ways and decorate the dinner table. But for everyday drinking, pouring wine into a glass water jug serves the purpose perfectly well. If you want to show off your bottle, you can always pour the wine back in before you serve it, a process known as double decanting. Opening a wine a few hours in advance to 'let it breathe' in the bottle is not very effective, since only a very small area of the liquid in the bottle is exposed to the air.

How long in advance should you decant your wine?

This depends on several things, including the age of the wine, its structure and balance, and your own drinking preferences. Broadly speaking, the older the wine, the more fragile it will be and the less time it will need in decanter before drinking. These are wines that you will decant shortly before serving, with the sole purpose of removing the wine from the accumulated tannins in the bottom of the bottle. If the wine is very old, you may want to avoid decanting altogether, to avoid exposing the wine to the air too soon. For aerating young wines, on the other hand, you can afford to experiment more. Young wines with high levels of tannin or acidity or oak (or all three) can improve over several hours in a jug or decanter. Be sure to taste the wine yourself when you first open the bottle to see how it changes with exposure to air.

If you find you've left it too late to decant a young wine that seems too tough to drink, don't panic. Decant it anyway, maybe twice, and then serve it in large glasses, allowing plenty of room for swirling the wine. This will allow the wine to open up in the glass. You can even pour the wine into glasses half an hour or so before you intend to drink it. Just remember that when you top up your glass, the new wine will be slightly different.

Choosing wine glasses

We have already seen that for tasting wine it is better to use a glass with a basic tulip shape (rather than a straight-sided or open 'V' shape). You will almost certainly find that as you pay more attention to tasting (and especially, smelling) the wines you drink, you will favour this shape of glass for all your drinking.

Beyond the basic shape and something that pleases you aesthetically, does the choice of wine glass make any difference to your drinking experience? Many people believe that it does. The main theory, expounded in particular by the glassware manufacturer, Riedel, is that the shape and size of the bowl of the glass will affect where the wine lands on your tongue, and also the speed at which it travels to get there. If you are as sceptical as I was when I first heard this, try experimenting for yourself with the same wine in different-shaped glasses and see the difference that it makes.

If you don't have a range of glasses at home, the next time you go to a restaurant ask if you can try your wine in two different glasses. Try a Bordeaux wine from a Burgundy glass, or Shiraz from a Champagne flute. You may be surprised (as was I) at just how much the same wine can vary in smell and taste across a range of glass shapes and sizes.

There are now glasses available to suit an astounding number of wine styles and grape varieties. Most of us will buy only a couple of different types of glassware, but it is certainly worth experimenting to find glasses that best suit the styles of wine you drink the most, or like the best.

Whatever glasses you choose, make sure there is always enough room in the bowl to allow you to swirl the wine to make the most of its aromas. In order to do this, fill glasses sparingly, leaving plenty of space between the wine and the top of the glass.

It is preferable to use a wine glass with a stem. You can now buy stemless wine glasses, but aside from the benefit that they are less likely to break, it is hard to see that they improve the drinking experience. Holding a glass by the stem makes it easier to move the wine in your glass and prevents the liquid being warmed by your hands.

Other things to consider when choosing glasses are the quality of the glass and the thickness of the rim. A rounder-edged glass will deliver a less satisfying experience than thin-rimmed crystal that forms a virtually imperceptible barrier between the wine and your lips.

> **Top tip**
> Keep wine glasses stored upright and away from strong smells, which they will absorb easily.

How to choose which wine to serve at home

If you need to be told what not to wear, you probably need to be told what not to drink. Some would have you believe that there is a right wine for every occasion and situation. If you prefer to let others choose your clothes or order you food in restaurants, then by all means let them choose the wine you drink as well. There are designer wines just as there are designer clothes and if you need brands, wine has those too. But if you are the sort of person who wants to take charge of your own decisions, who wants to be informed, in short, if you are the sort of person who has bought this book, the good news is that there are few rules about which wine to serve. Below are the conventional rules on the serving order of wines. But as with all rules, they are made to be broken. Once you work out which wines you like, your decision about which wines to serve will be as personal as the food you cook or the clothes you wear.

The order of serving different wines

The usual rules for the order of serving wines are:

- white before red
- dry before sweet
- young before old.

The main considerations for pre-dinner drinks are that the wine should be light and refreshing. Choose a crisp wine, ideally fairly low in alcohol. An exception to the low alcohol rule is Fino sherry. The tangy flavour is the perfect appetite sharpener (and it's also great with salty snacks).

The rules of white before red and dry before sweet are intended to help the palate adjust to the increasing demands of tannins and sugar in the wine. In the same way that you would find it hard to go back to eating olives after chocolate, sweetness in wine stays in the mouth for some time, making it hard to go back to dry wines. With a long enough pause, however, it's quite possible to go from sweet to dry and back to sweet again.

White wines are well suited to drinking first; they tend to be lighter and their higher acidity compared to reds sharpens the appetite. They also usually match the weight of lighter first-course dishes. The stronger flavours in red wine tend to suit more strongly flavoured food, such as richer, meat-based dishes.

Like most rules, though, there are exceptions. For example, the rationale of serving young wine before old is that we will appreciate the subtleties of the older wine after the brash simplicity of the younger one. In reality, we'd probably appreciate the older, more delicate wine best of all at the start of the meal, when our palates are fresh and uncluttered by other flavours. More often, the reason the old wine is served at the end of the meal is simply because it's the best wine – a case of saving the best until last.

Similarly, it's fine to break the 'white before red' rule. White wines can happily follow reds, in the right context. Don't be afraid to experiment with the wine *you* feel best matches the flavours in your food.

Try this

An experiment suggested by Tim Hanni MW – on the next five occasions you drink wine with food, choose a wine that you like, but that you think will match least well with the food you are eating. How do you rate the experience? Did you still enjoy the food? Did you still enjoy the wine? For most people, drinking a wine they like is more important to their enjoyment of food and wine than trying to match the right wine with the right flavours in their food.

12

understanding wine labels

In this chapter you will learn:
- how to tell from the label if a wine is sweet or dry
- the meaning of Premier Cru and Grand Cru
- how to make sense of German wine labels
- which words you can ignore on a label.

What's in a label?

A wine's label is its only obvious point of difference on the shelf. Here is the information you should be able to glean from it:

- the country where the wine was produced
- the country where the wine was bottled
- the region or sub-region of production
- the legally designated quality level
- the percentage alcohol by volume
- the volume of wine in the bottle
- in most cases, the year of production.

To the above list you can add the name of the predominant grape variety for almost every wine from a new world wine-producing nation. In Europe, though, it is far less common to see the name of the grapes used to make the wine, especially in the more traditional wine-producing regions. Refer to Chapter 03 for information on the grape varieties that make up some of the better-known of these wines.

It would be really helpful if there were some sort of international standard for quality in wine, but unfortunately, there isn't. In fact, there are even different quality standards from one wine region to the next within the same country, or even the same region. A Grand Cru in Saint-Emilion is not the same as a Grand Cru of the Médoc, although both are regions of Bordeaux. A Grand Cru in Bordeaux is not the same as a Grand Cru in Burgundy. And in Alsace, it means something else again. The tendency of old world wine producers to focus on the details from a very local perspective, rather than a broader one, makes it difficult for those of us with a broad choice of wine to distinguish meaningful differences between them. The aim of this chapter is to give you the best chance of working out how a wine will taste from looking at the label.

Some words you can ignore

Not everything on a wine label is useful. Like much packaging, some of the words are just designed to sell the bottle. Here are some of the more common pufferies that you might find on a bottle (and some of them appear in several languages):

- reserve
- special
- tradition

- selection
- cuvée XYZ.

These words are useful to distinguish one wine from another from the same producer, but do not in themselves tell you anything about the wine's qualities. Another misleading and commonly seen word is 'supérieur' (or 'superiore' on Italian labels). Occasionally this means there is something genuinely better about the wine, but in most cases it is merely a sign that the wine has slightly more alcoholic strength than the same bottle without the 'superior' mention.

Sweet or dry?

Many, if not most, sweet wines do not say they are sweet on the label. If you are buying wine in a shop or a restaurant, a wine that is always sweet should be highlighted as such. (If all you have to judge by is the sight of the bottle, and you suspect the wine might be sweet, look at the colour of the liquid. If it is a deep, yellow-gold colour, there is a good chance it is sweet).

It is much more difficult to know if a wine will be sweet if it is only medium sweet, or if it is sweet in some years but not others. Look out for the words for dry, medium and sweet (noted in the foreign language Glossary at the back of the book). If there is no mention on the front label, you will need to rely on the notes on the back label, a knowledgeable shop assistant or wine waiter, or you will need some knowledge of the wine producer. It also helps to know the regions where this is likely to be a problem (see Alsace and Germany, below).

French labels

The most important quality designation in France is Appellation d'Origine Contrôlée, often seen abbreviated to AOC, or AC. This nationally regulated system is applied to many foodstuffs, not just to wine. This is the most important category for wine classification, accounting for more wine on the shelves today than any other. There are hundreds of different ACs in France, ranging in size from single vineyard plots to an entire region (such as AC Bordeaux). Producers wishing to use the term on their wine must comply with rules that govern everything from the varieties of grapes that may be planted to the way the vines are pruned. There are limits on the quantity of fruit that may be harvested.

Because an AC can be granted to a tiny area, this may be the only thing that is mentioned on the label. For example, a wine from the Grand Cru of Clos de la Roche in Morey St-Denis, in Burgundy's Côte de Nuits, might be labelled only 'Clos de la Roche Grand Cru', and underneath, 'Appellation Clos de la Roche Contrôlée'. You may search in vain to find the word 'Burgundy' (or even the French equivalent, Bourgogne) on the bottle, or the name of the village. Unfortunately, it's up to you to know.

A step below the AC level is the small group of wines labelled VDQS, which stands for Vin Délimité de Qualité Supérieure. In some regions, producers may decide to opt for greater freedom of choice in the wines they make and forego the AC system in order to use different grape varieties, or to produce at higher yields than is permitted under the AC system. Below the AC rank is the increasingly interesting category of Vins de Pays, regional wines that are produced throughout France. These wines have more flexibility in their production methods and will often state grape varieties on their labels – something that is forbidden in most of the French AC regions.

If you've never heard of any of these distinctions, don't worry, because they are very likely to be changing any time. As this book goes to press, INAO, the body that controls all the appellations of origin, has declared its intention to abandon the old acronyms in favour of some new ones (just to keep us all on our toes). AOC could become AOP, the 'P' indicating that the appellation of origin will be protected ('Protégée'), rather than merely controlled. The Vins de Pays category would be renamed 'protected geographical region' (Indication Géographique Protégée). The most basic current category of wine, table wine (vin de table) would be renamed Vignobles de France (vineyards of France). As none of these changes has happened yet, however, I'll stick to the current convention of ACs here.

Grand Cru or Premier Cru (or Premier Grand Cru)?

These quality terms, which translate literally as 'Great Growth', 'First Growth', and 'First Great Growth' are bandied around rather too freely in some regions, but do have real meaning in others. You will see in the sections below how to interpret these terms. The important thing to bear in mind is that not everything labelled *grand* really is great. For example, you can always ignore any label that professes greatness in the form of Grand Vin (Grand Vin de Bourgogne, Grand Vin de Bordeaux, and so on). This assertion tells you nothing more than that the wine comes from this region of origin.

Bordeaux

Bordeaux wines are identified by their individual appellations, which relate to the place the grapes are grown. In addition, there are several different quality classifications which you will see noted on the label. These classifications attach to the property (invariably called a *château*, even if it is rarely actually a grand castle), rather than to a patch of land.

The oldest Bordeaux ranking is the classification of the **Médoc**, which was drawn up in 1855. This identified the top 60 properties according to the prices their wines were achieving in the market at this time. All were situated in the Médoc area, with the exception of Château Haut-Brion, in the Bordeaux suburb of Pessac-Léognan. This classification is still in use today and, although the prices of the wines from the various châteaux reflect the quality of the wines being made today, they are still ranked in the same order, into First, Second, Third, Fourth and Fifth growths ('Crus'). These wines will be labelled with the appellation of the commune where the grapes were grown, plus the words 'Grand Cru Classé', or 'Grand Cru Classé en 1855'. Sometimes there will also be a mention of the ranking of the château: for example, 'Premier Grand Cru Classé', although this particular (*premier*) distinction will only be seen on the labels of the top five red wines: Château Margaux, Château Lafite, Château Latour, Château Mouton-Rothschild and Château Haut-Brion. The 1855 classification is only for red wines and has only ever been altered once, to promote Château Mouton-Rothschild to a first growth.

A further classification, beneath the Grands Crus Classés, that you may see on the label of a wine from the Médoc is Cru Bourgeois, Cru Bourgeois Supérieur, or Cru Bourgeois Exceptionnel. These ascending quality rankings encompass hundreds more estates of the region. This classification was annulled by the government in 2007, but looks set to be re-introduced in the near future.

The sweet wines of **Sauternes** were classified at the same time as the 1855 Médoc classification, with the best wines divided into First Growths (Premiers Crus), Second Growths (Deuxièmes Crus) and, at the top, one Superior First Growth, Château d'Yquem. Any wine labelled Sauternes will be sweet.

In 1959, a classification was introduced for the best wines of the **Graves** (Pessac-Léognan) district. Wines were classified by property and by colour, so a property might be a classed growth for red but not white wines, and vice versa. There are 13 red wines classified and nine dry whites. There is no hierarchy within this classification. Wines awarded in this classification will be labelled 'Grand Cru Classé de Graves'.

In contrast to the relatively static classifications of the Left Bank, over on the Right Bank, in **Saint-Emilion**, the classification of red winemaking properties is reviewed every ten years. Châteaux are ranked into Grands Crus Classés (which number 50 plus), and 13 Premier Grands Crus Classés. The most recent classification was in 2006, but due to disputes over the lack of impartiality of the judgement, it has been suspended. Growers have reverted temporarily to the 1996 classification (so they still have something to put on their label).

There is more than just a changing and cancelled classification to confuse us in Saint-Emilion. In addition to the Grands Crus Classés there is another, much larger, classification, that of Saint-Emilion Grand Cru. There is nothing very great about these properties, which account for a greater vineyard area than those accorded the simple Saint-Emilion appellation.

Despite their high status and prices, there is no official classification for the wines of **Pomerol**.

Burgundy

Grand Cru is the highest appellation for any wine in Burgundy. Here, *grand* is very often great, although the skill of the producer always plays a particularly significant role in the production of great wine in this part of the world. Grand Cru wines represent a tiny part of the wine produced in the region. Next comes Premier Cru. Both of these classifications usually apply to quite small sites. The lower down the designated quality scale you go, the larger the area tends to be. Next down from Premier Cru come the village appellations (for example, AC Beaune), where grapes can be sourced from any vineyards in the region of a particular village. Finally, come the broader, regional appellations, which might encompass grapes grown in any village in a larger area (AC Côte de Nuits-Villages, for example), or, at the broadest level, anywhere in the Burgundy region (AC Bourgogne).

Chablis is a part of Burgundy and has the same style of appellation system, with Grands Crus, Premiers Crus and, at the village level, simple AC Chablis. **Beaujolais**, also a part of

Burgundy, has no Premier or Grand Crus, but does have ten 'Crus', named after the villages where the grapes are grown. These Crus have their own appellations.

Alsace

There are two main appellations to be concerned with in Alsace: Alsace and Alsace Grand Cru. However, some of the best wines are not called Grand Cru because some producers have opted out and refuse to acknowledge the classification's validity (one of the arguments being that when the Grand Cru sites were drawn up, political considerations sometimes took precedence over quality, so every village was awarded one).

Many Alsace wines have some sweetness, although it is not usually mentioned on the label. If a wine is labelled 'Vendanges Tardives', meaning late harvest, it will probably not be dry. If a wine is labelled 'Sélection de Grains Nobles' it will be sweet, made from late-harvested berries affected by noble rot. If you like wines from Alsace, it pays to get to know which producers produce drier wines and which ones like to leave some residual sweetness.

Champagne

Champagne wine labels are straightforward to understand. If a wine has no year on it (which is the case of most Champagne), it is a blend of the crop from several years and termed non-vintage (sometimes seen on a label as 'NV'). If a year is noted on Champagne, this is vintage Champagne, sourced from a single year's fruit.

Grand Cru and Premier Cru are sometimes seen on Champagne labels. These terms refer to the villages where the grapes grow. If all of the grapes in a wine come from Grand Cru vineyards, the Champagne can be labelled as such.

Most Champagne is dry, labelled Brut. Although Sec translates into English as 'Dry', Champagne labelled thus will be sweeter than dry, and certainly less dry than one labelled Brut. Demi-Sec is sweeter still, and the sweetest (though little seen) category is Doux. A further label you might see is Extra Brut, or Extra Dry, which means that the wine has had no added sugar (unlike Brut Champagne, which will always have some residual sweetness from the *dosage* used in its production – see Chapter 05 for more about how Champagne is made).

German labels

France may have a lot of classifications, but it is Germany that wins the prize for the world's most confusing wine labels. Few countries provide such a wealth of information on the label and still fail to address in plain English (or even German) whether the liquid in the bottle will be sweet, dry, or somewhere in between. But although it's often difficult, it is usually possible to work out more or less what you are going to be getting with German wine. It just takes a little more effort.

Starting at the bottom of the ladder, the most basic German wines are Tafelwein (table wine) and Landwein (country wine). Qualitätswein (or QbA) is higher quality wine that must be made from riper grapes from a specified region. All of these categories of wine can be chaptalized, meaning that winemakers can add sugar to the grape must to increase the potential alcoholic strength of their wine before fermentation. To make things easier for consumers (though you can be the judge of this), there are now two additional categories within QbA: Classic and Selection. These names are intended to be an indication (if not a very helpfully explicit one) that the wines will taste *essentially* dry – although they may still have some residual sugar. The term 'Selection' is a step up from 'Classic' in terms of quality.

The higher level Qualitätswein mit Prädikat (or QmP) wines are made from riper grapes that are not chaptalized and usually harvested later than grapes destined for QbA wines. This traditional quality classification system of German wine law is based around the sweetness (ripeness) of the grapes. There are designated wine regions and sites in Germany, but the defining character of the wine will always be as much about the ripeness of the grapes as anything else. Wines are ranked according to the level of potential alcohol (in other words, the level of sugar) in the grapes. In ascending order of sweetness these are:

- Kabinett
- Spätlese
- Auslese
- Beerenauslese
- Trockenbeerenauslese
- Eiswein.

The first three of these can be dry, medium-dry, or sweet. Dry and medium-dry wines will be labelled Trocken or Halbtrocken or Feinherb. Each of the above categories will have progressively higher levels of richness. In the case of dry wines, the categories will have progressively more alcohol, since more of the grapes' sugar has been fermented. Traditionally, all of these wines were made sweet, but an increasing proportion of Kabinett, Spätlese and Auslese wines are now being made in fully dry or off-dry styles. The last three categories will always be sweet. 'Beeren' refers to berries, usually affected by botrytis. 'Trockenbeeren' refers to botrytized berries, which appear dry (trocken) on the vine. And Eiswein is made from grapes left on the vines to freeze.

Frustrated by the lack of clarity over quality that has resulted from the traditional classifications, the association of the top 200 German producers, the VDP, decided to introduce its own rules. These rules are still being developed, but you may find the classifications and symbols outlined below on wine labels from producers who belong to the VDP. This is signified on the bottle by the letters 'VDP' above an eagle and a bunch of grapes.

In a move to re-establish the importance of vineyard sites, the VDP re-introduced the idea of site classification. The top sites (similar in quality terms to Premiers Crus in Burgundy) are called Erste Lage, or 'First Sites'. The words Erste Lage are not permitted on a label, but can be seen symbolized on a bottle as a number one next to a stylized bunch of grapes.

The concept of Erste Lage applies to dry and sweet wines. For dry wines with less than nine grams per litre residual sugar, the VDP introduced a new category, Grosses Gewächs, or 'Great Growths'. This is abbreviated to 'GG' on a label. In the Rheingau region, they use a different name, Erstes Gewächs, and the wines may contain a little more residual sugar, but they also taste dry.

Italian labels

Italian labels are relatively simple, if sometimes sparse, in the information they provide. The categories of wine are, in descending order of greatness:

- DOCG Denominazione di Origine Controllata e Garantita
- DOC Denominazione di Origine Controllata

- IGT – Indicazione Geografica Tipica
- VdT – Vino da Tavola.

Note that there are many very high-quality IGT wines in Italy, made by producers who do not wish to be constrained by the restrictions of the DOC rules.

The names of the DOCs often include grape varieties, as well as the region the wines come from, for example, Moscato d'Asti DOCG, which is wine made from Muscat grapes grown in the Asti region.

Spanish labels

Most wine you will see from Spain is classified DO or DOCa, initials that stand for Denominación de Origen and Denominación de Origen Calificada, respectively. The latter category has only been awarded to two regions, Rioja and Priorat.

Other classifications you may see on the label are:

- DO Pago – Denominación de Origen Pago – for single estate wines
- VCIG – Vino de Calidad con Indicación Geografica – a step up from VdlT
- VdlT – Vino de la Tierra – like French vins de pays
- VdM – Vino de Mesa – table wine.

13

buying wine

In this chapter you will learn:
- the best places to buy wine
- how to buy wine in restaurants with confidence
- how to know if a wine is corked
- how to buy wine as a gift for different occasions
- how to be a 'green' wine shopper.

Options for buying wine

For most of us, the easiest way to buy wine is at the supermarket, and the selection can be excellent. But if you are interested in exploring a particular wine region, or trying to find a particular wine, you will probably want to visit a specialist wine merchant. Most specialist wine shops have staff who are actively interested in wine and will be pleased to help you with your selection. They will usually have had the opportunity to taste many of the wines in the shop, or to know someone who has. When you are faced with this situation, it is especially helpful to be able to explain the style of wine you like, as this will help you to expand your drinking repertoire. You'll also often have the chance to taste wines in the shop, so make the most of the opportunity to do so.

If you are buying wine in quantities of 12 bottles or more, it can make sense to buy mail order. Give your name and address to a few wine merchants and you will soon be inundated with offers to buy the latest releases. Many wine merchants organize excellent tastings themed by region, which is another way to try before you buy. The internet makes it even easier to stay up to date with what is on offer, as you will usually have the option to receive information by email.

If you don't have the confidence to dive in and make your own selections blind from a list, there are numerous opportunities to let someone else help you, or make the decisions for you until you find your feet. Look out for cellar plans that help you to select wine on the basis of how much you want to spend, the styles of wine you like; how many bottles you want to buy; or when you want to drink them. Wine merchants can often offer storage facilities for bottles that deserve keeping.

One of the ways to make sure you have access to wines you like is to buy them before they are physically available. This is known as *en primeur* buying, and is becoming increasingly common for wines that are in highest demand. You can buy *en primeur* wines from Bordeaux, Burgundy, the Rhône Valley, Piedmont and Germany, for example. Buying wine in this way provides useful cash flow for the producer and can save you money if the price of the wine is likely to rise after its release. When you buy wine like this you are buying it 'in bond', which means you pay the price of the wine excluding excise duty and tax. These will be due when the wine is delivered and will be payable at the current rate. If you do buy wine in this way, it pays to use a reputable merchant with a history of selling wine in this way; in recent years the collapse of several sellers of *en primeur* wines has led to buyers losing their money.

Buying wine at a winery is a fun thing to do, especially if drinking the wine recalls memories of the place you bought it. It can also save you money and give you access to wines that might not be available at home. Think about the conditions you have for transporting the wine home (the back of a boiling hot car is less than ideal) and remember that if you spit rather than swallow when making holiday wine purchases, you will probably be making a better choice.

Buying wine in bars and restaurants

The bar or restaurant wine purchase is potentially the most stressful of wine-buying occasions. You probably have a fair idea what sort of food you're likely to be served, but in most cases, the wine list comes as a lot more of a surprise – and usually an expensive one. In the UK, wine prices are commonly marked up by 300 per cent, so not only are you faced with a list of strange wines, but you have to pay way over the usual shop price. This makes it all the more important to have good strategies in place to manage the wine-buying experience.

Deciphering the wine list

The quality, style and choice on wine lists are as varied as the restaurants where you find them. Wines are usually grouped by colour, price, sparkling and sweet, half bottles and larger sizes. Some are helpfully arranged by style. So where should you start when making your choice of wine?

The traditional view is to start your search by thinking about the food you are going to eat. But you're probably better off starting with the style of wine you like. Think about it: even if you find the perfect wine and food flavour match for one dish, what about all the others? Even if you are only two people, the chances are you'll be eating different food. With larger groups, things get more complicated, and you can never be sure, even if the menu is very descriptive, just how the balance of flavours will be for each person's food.

Here are some approaches to looking at any wine list you are presented with.

House wine

As a general rule, beware of unidentified house wine. It could be absolutely anything and, although you'd hope a restaurant would choose a house wine it could be proud of, it's sadly often not the case. Unless you'd be happy to pay £15 in a shop for a bottle just labelled 'white' or 'red', why would you do it in a restaurant? If the waiter can't tell you what the wine is, it's probably not very good. On the other hand, if the waiter is enthusiastic about the house wine, it's probably worth a try. The quality of house wine very often depends on the type of restaurant you are in. A high-quality restaurant will probably have a good house wine.

Look for the familiar

It might sound a bit boring, but it's always a good idea to get a handle on a wine list by trying to find a wine, or style of wine, you know and like. Check the price to compare it to what you would buy it for in a shop. If this is what you want to order, obviously you can do that. Alternatively, you can now use this knowledge to help you to understand to what degree you can use the skills of your waiter.

Use the waiter

Ask the waiter, or wine waiter if there is one, if he or she knows the wine you've chosen – and ask for an opinion on it. This will tell you two things: first, it will tell you whether the waiter knows the wine list (and therefore, whether you can trust the help on offer, or whether you are on your own; you may be surprised that many waiters know very little about wine); second, you will know if the waiter shares or understands your taste. If your waiter knows nothing about any of the wines, you might ask if there is someone who does, as many restaurants have one or more waiters who are better informed about the wines they serve than others. If you are lucky and find the waiter passes this first test of actually knowing the wine you are asking about, you can feel more confident to ask further questions to establish if there are other wines in this style that you might try. Perhaps you might like to try a similar wine from another country, or to experiment with a more expensive wine in a similar style. If you can't find a wine you know, ask the waiter to recommend something in the style of something you do know you like. Don't be afraid to use waiters; it's their job and in almost every case they'll be happy you asked.

Know the style of wine you like

See Chapters 06 and 07 to understand the types of wines you are likely to enjoy. This will make things a lot easier from the outset. Also, make the most of the knowledge you already have – you probably already know a lot more than you think you do.

Don't forget half bottles!

Halves are a brilliant alternative to buying wine by the glass – and the best way of ensuring the wine you are buying is freshly opened. It's also a good way to try something new. As wine tends to mature faster in a smaller bottle (because there is more air in the bottle relative to the volume of wine), you can also have the chance of enjoying a more mature wine. Halves are useful if you are with several people who want to drink different wines, or if you are dining alone. They are also useful for styles of wine you'll typically drink in smaller quantities, such as sweet wines.

Look for grape varieties

Many wine lists are now ordered according to grape varieties. Even if they are not, you should be able to ask the waiter to point out wines made from the varieties you like. Remember, some grape varieties are a lot more reliable than others, and consistently show the varietal characters you will recognize, for example:

Reliable white varieties:

- Sauvignon Blanc
- Riesling
- Grüner Veltliner.

Reliable red varieties:

- Cabernet Sauvignon
- Shiraz/Syrah.

New world wines are a safer bet

Whether or not you have a preference for European wines, you'll often find wines from the new world more reliable buys on restaurant lists, as there is less vintage variation from one year to the next than for old world wine regions. This is particularly true at the cheaper price levels on a wine list.

Classics – do your homework

If you think you're likely to be ordering something expensive from a classic wine region, it pays to do your homework in advance. These wines are invariably highly vintage dependent and quality varies from one producer to the next. Many restaurants publish their wine lists online, and you can see where to find up-to-date information on the vintages of classic regions in the Taking it Further section at the back of this book. If you can't remember the details, but want to drink something special from the old world, quiz the waiter about the differences between the wines and vintages. Anybody who knows his or her stuff will be more than happy to wax lyrical about the differences between one wine and the next – and to stick within the price range you suggest. Be especially careful with red Burgundy wines: quality can be very variable.

Sweet or dry

A good wine list should tell you if a wine is anything other than dry, but you can ask. Always check if the wine will be sweet or dry if you have chosen anything from Germany or Alsace, Chenin Blanc from the Loire Valley, or anything made from Riesling grapes. But don't be put off by sweeter styles: some can be excellent with food.

Don't forget unusual wines or combinations of wine

Especially for aperitifs, it's good to look at the wine list. You might find a half bottle of something interesting (such as sherry or sweet wine), or a bottle that can be enjoyed with a starter and cheese.

Be adventurous

Although it can be a useful strategy to look for the familiar, it pays to seek out unfamiliar names if you are looking for a bargain. It's much more difficult for a restaurant to charge a huge mark-up on an unknown wine than it is for the names we're all familiar with (Bordeaux, Rioja, Burgundy and so on). Conversely, some wines that are always high in price, such as big Champagne names, can sometimes be relatively well priced in restaurants, simply because few people would be prepared to pay very high mark-ups for wines which they know are expensive in the first place.

Compare the prices

Pricing policies in restaurants vary considerably, so although the fixed percentage mark-up across all wines is common, it's not universal. Often the mark-ups are lower on more expensive wines, so it's better value to trade up. Fixed-price mark-ups are a welcome trend for wine lovers. If you can find a wine you know the value of, you can get an idea of the pricing policy of the restaurant – or if you're bold enough, you could always ask!

Unknown wines (or why a wine list rarely has all the wines you see in the shops)

One extra confusion of buying wine in restaurants is that you will frequently come across wines you'll never have seen anywhere else. Some of these (at the expensive end of the wine list) will be low-quantity, high-end wines that are only distributed in any volume to restaurants. But there are many other wines at the cheaper end of the list that you will never see in a shop. You will look in vain for the familiar high street names in most restaurants. One reason for this practice is so that you can't compare the restaurant price with the price you'd find it for in your local supermarket (in which case, you would be less likely to buy it at an inflated restaurant price).

If this makes it sound like restaurants are out to rip you off on wine, it's not necessarily the case. Restaurants need to charge a mark-up on wine, just as they do on food. However, it does make an even stronger case for making sure you get the service you are paying for. But even if restaurants do count on making a sizeable percentage of their profits from the wine list, there will usually be some bargains and some interesting wines to be found on any list.

Buying wine by the glass

Compared to buying a whole bottle, buying a glass of wine seems a less risky purchase. But drink for drink, the prices are usually the same, so you should expect the quality of the wine to be just as good as a full bottle. The advantage of buying wine by the glass is that you can try different wines without committing to drinking a whole bottle of something you might not really like. Any place that has an interesting list of wines by the glass is likely to take its wine seriously, and this is becoming a welcome option in an increasing number of restaurants. But there are things to be careful of when you buy by the glass. The major hazard is that you are more likely to be finishing off a leftover bottle than having a bottle opened freshly for you.

Professional equipment to keep wines fresh is expensive and few places have it. But there is a lot you can do for yourself to work out how fresh the wine is. Have a look at how open bottles are stored, and how much wine is being sold. They may be sealed with one of the preservation systems described in Chapter 14, or the bottles might simply be re-sealed with the cork and put back on the bar. Ask how long the bottle has been open. If it's longer than a few hours, pick something else – or ask for something fresher. Wines deteriorate at different rates once they have been opened (see Chapter 14), but if you are looking for a wine that is aromatic and delicate, you'll be unlikely to enjoy a bottle that was opened six hours ago. The wines that keep the least well once opened are old wines, delicate white wines and wines (red or white) with low levels of natural acidity.

Tasting the wine

Once you've ordered your wine, the waiter should open it in front of you (if you have ordered a bottle) and should always ask you if you want to taste the wine (although he or she may do this for you in smarter establishments). There are few things to be dogmatic about in wine, but here the answer should always be 'Yes' and *never* the often heard 'Oh no, I'm sure it's fine'. Why? Because unless you taste the wine, you can never be sure it is fine. Which brings us to the next point: how can you tell if the wine is alright?

Corked wine

The main problem you are likely to encounter in wines sealed with a natural cork is 'corked' wine. This term is a bit of a misnomer, since the fault has nothing to do with pieces of stray cork getting into the glass. If this happens, it will not affect the taste of your wine. If the flavour of cork itself were detrimental to the flavour if wine, it would spoil all wine sealed with a cork, since the liquid is in constant contact with cork until it is opened.

Corked wine is something else entirely. It is a wine fault caused by a chemical that has infiltrated the wine, almost always via the cork. This can happen during the production process of the cork or in the place the wine is made or bottled. Detectable in minuscule amounts – just a couple of parts per billion – the presence of this chemical can ruin a wine, making it smell and taste musty, dusty and flat. The smell is likened to damp cardboard and is really quite unpleasant. The smell will also be detectable on the underside of the cork, which is why waiters often smell the cork after opening the bottle, as this is the first clue that there may be a problem with the wine. However, this in itself is not usually sufficient to confirm that a wine is corked. It needs to be smelled or tasted to know for sure.

It is hard to familiarize yourself with the smell of corked, or 'corky' wines, since there are relatively few badly corked wines (only one or two per cent of bottles, by most estimates), but it is a problem that can afflict any wine, from the most basic to the most expensive. Anyone who is serving you wine should be familiar with the potential problem, though, so if in doubt, ask for a second opinion.

One of the problems of a wine that is corked is that there are varying degrees of corkiness, so a wine may be badly corked (which you will probably spot), or only slightly corked. In the case of the latter, it is very hard to be sure if the wine is faulty or not. If the wine is one that you know, you may find that the fruit is just not as expressive as it usually is, which is a symptom of corked wine. Note that the problem is exacerbated by exposure to air, so if you feel a wine may be corked, but you are not quite sure at first, your waiter should understand if you only notice the problem by the end of your first glass.

All corked wine should be replaced without question. It is a very rude waiter who will argue otherwise. If you are with a large enough party that you will be ordering two bottles, you could always ask for a second bottle if you are unsure about the quality of the first, and compare the two.

What if the wine is sealed with a screwcap?

Rejoice! It's highly unlikely that it will have any faults. Screwcaps have become a valued closure for high-quality wines (especially white wines) for their ability to keep wines fresh and free from cork taint.

Other wine faults

If you have ordered wine by the glass, the most likely fault is that the wine will be oxidized, or stale, because it comes from a bottle that has been left open too long.

It's useful to familiarize yourself with the taste of oxidized (stale) wine (see below), as you are, unfortunately, quite likely to be served some at some point. Even good restaurants are guilty of this rather sloppy practice. I ordered two different wines by the glass at an expensive London restaurant recently. Both cost upwards of £10 per glass; both were oxidized. I called the waiter over and told him the wines were not in good condition. His answer: 'But they were freshly opened – yesterday.' More proof that you need to take control of your drinking.

Try this

Familiarize yourself with the smell and taste of stale (oxidized) wine at home to avoid having to buy it when you are out. The next time you open a bottle of wine, make a tasting note. Instead of finishing the bottle, leave some wine in the bottom of the open bottle and leave it open for a day or so. Taste it again periodically. You will notice that the fruit flavours and aromas you noted when you first tasted the wine become more indistinct. You may also notice that these pleasant aromas have been replaced by less pleasant ones. These are the rancid, dull, often vinegary aromas of oxidation that you need to fix in your mind for the next time you are served wine that has been open too long in a bar or restaurant. If you can't tell the difference, leave the bottle open another day and try again. To make this easier, buy two bottles of the same wine. Once the remains of the first bottle have been sitting around for a while, open the second bottle and compare the two. It should be easy to see the difference. The more tasting experience you have, the easier it will be to know what to expect from the flavours in the wine you buy – and the less willing you will be to drink tired wine.

It can also happen that wine can oxidize in bottle before it is opened. A wine that has aged badly, or is just too old to drink, will taste flat and dull. Old wines oxidize naturally, but younger wines can become damaged from excessive exposure to heat and light, or through faulty bottling or closures. Oxidized white wine will be deep in colour; oxidized red wine will be dull and fading, or browning. White wine may have nutty, sherry-like aromas. If a wine is very old, or if this is part of the style of the wine (sherries, for example), this type of oxidation is not necessarily a fault. But if a wine less than five years old is displaying this sort of character, it should give you cause for concern.

What should you do if you just don't like the taste of the wine you've been given? You shouldn't really have to deal with nasty surprises when you buy wine in a restaurant. If you don't know what style of wine you are buying, ask the wine waiter. He or she should know, or at least be able to find out for you. If the wine isn't how you expected it to be, ask the waiter to taste it for you to check it is in good condition.

Decanting wine

If the waiter asks if you'd like the wine decanted and you don't know, you can always ask the question back: 'Would you decant it?' Or, you can taste the wine first, and then decide. See Chapter 11 for more on when to decant wine. The restaurant should offer to decant the wine if there is a significant sediment in the bottle, since once this is disturbed by pouring, it can impart bitter flavours to the wine (next time you see some sediment, taste it to see for yourself!). The other main reason to decant is to aerate the wine, so that it 'opens up' to enable you to enjoy it over the course of your meal. Most wine sold in restaurants is of recent vintages that would probably benefit from decanting, so if in doubt, say yes if offered the choice of decanting a young wine. And decanting is not just for red wines and not just for expensive wines, either. Many white wines can be improved by decanting. If you are not given the option, don't be afraid to ask your waiter to decant the wine into something (it doesn't have to be a fancy decanter, either). If you feel your wine would benefit from a little air, you can always request a glass jug to pour it into.

Chilling the wine

The temperature you prefer for your wine is up to you. You can read more about serving temperatures for different wines in Chapter 11. Experiment to see what you like. If you feel your red wine is too warm, ask your waiter to put it on ice to cool down for a few minutes before pouring it. Restaurants often keep wines in less than ideal conditions and, especially in summer, red wines are frequently served at kitchen, rather than cellar, temperature.

Restaurant rules – remember who is the boss!

In a restaurant, you should *always* be able to ask the waiter:

- Do you know this wine?
- I know I like *x* style of wine: can you recommend something similar from your list?
- Is this wine ready to drink?
- Can you taste this and tell me if you think it is okay?
- Do you think this wine is corked?
- Please can you decant the wine.
- Please chill the wine.
- Please take the wine off ice to warm it up a little.
- Please leave the bottle on the table.

Choosing wine for other people

It can be a worry to buy wine for other people. How can you know what they'll like? If in doubt, go with a wine you know *you* like. Below are a few more suggestions for how to think about choosing wine for others.

Special occasions

A dinner party

Your choice here depends on how well you know your hosts. If you know them well, find out what they like to drink. You can refer to Chapter 07 to find similar examples of wines in styles they might like. If you don't know your hosts well, think about taking a favourite wine of your own. If you are not confident that other people will share your taste, or you want to buy something special, a safe bet for a white wine is Champagne or white Burgundy (including Chablis). For reds, you won't go wrong with a Syrah from the northern Rhône, Chianti Classico, or Rioja.

Buying for wine enthusiasts

It can be intimidating buying wine for someone who knows more about wine than you do. Here are a few interesting and quite special wines to appeal to the drinker who's tried everything. For whites, choose Albariño from Spain, Grüner

Veltliner from Austria, Assyrtiko from Santorini or dry Furmint from Hungary. For reds, think about a Tannat from Uruguay, a Blaufränkisch from Austria, or Pinot Noir from Chile's up-and-coming Leyda Valley.

Drinks party

Pick a wine to match the atmosphere you are trying to create. Fizz is always festive and few people will refuse a glass of Champagne. If your budget does not stretch to such luxuries, make sure you choose something light and refreshing. Don't forget rosé, which is now appreciated by just about everyone. For reds, choose something light that slips down easily. Think about the weather outside and the time of year, as well. Our tastes change with the seasons. A rich, spicy red will always work better in winter than it will in the middle of summer.

Picnics and barbecues

If you are outside, especially if the atmosphere is smoky, you are not going to appreciate the finer points of any wine. Avoid delicate whites, or anything too rich, heavy, or oaky. Instead, choose something zingy but light, to provide simple, quaffing refreshment without excessive alcohol, such as Australian Sémillon, South African Sauvignon Blanc, white Bordeaux or a good Pinot Grigio from Italy. Most rosé is good for outdoor occasions. For red wines, choose a light red that can be cooled for a summer picnic, such as Valpolicella from Italy, red Sancerre, or Beaujolais. For a red wine to match smoky, spicy barbecue flavours, try a Zinfandel from the USA or a juicy wine from the southern Rhône.

Family gathering

There's nothing better than sharing delicious wine with loved ones. Times like these call for crowd-pleasing, uncontroversial wines. Choose fruit over structure. For white wines, this means avoiding anything too dry and anything with excessively sharp acidity. Instead, favour wines with bright fruit and aromas. For red wines, think smooth. No harsh tannins and lots of nice, soft, ripe fruit will please everyone. New world wines fit these criteria most easily (New Zealand Pinot Noir and Californian reds, for example), although Rioja is a reliable family favourite. For special occasions like Christmas or birthdays, see if you can find a wine in a larger format, such as a magnum.

How to be a green wine shopper

Organic wine

Wines made from organically grown grapes are rapidly entering the mainstream, as demand for all things organic continues to grow and the quality of these wines rises. Although there is a bewildering number of certifying organic bodies, the basic requirement of all of them is that organic grapes need to be grown without use of synthetic fertilizers, herbicides, fungicides or pesticides.

Wine has been relatively slow to follow the spectacular growth in organic food, possibly because of negative associations with the quality of some organic wine in the past. Strictly speaking, organic wine doesn't exist – at least, not in the European Union, which only legislates organic production of grapes, not wine. There are a few organic wines in the USA, but the reason for their low number is that producers of organic wine are forbidden from using any sulphur dioxide in the winery, something that is anathema to most winemakers, since sulphur protects wine from both oxidation and bacterial spoilage.

The good news for those who wish to avoid grapes grown with synthetic chemicals is that there is now a huge selection of really top-quality organic wines on offer. It's often said that organically grown wines come with a hefty price tag attached. It's true that farming organically is riskier in many parts of the world and some of the wines do cost more. But it is hard to quantify the costs of organic viticulture, especially when the cost of a wine is about so much more than the practices used to grow the grapes. Ease of applying organic principles depends to a large extent on where grapes are grown and what sorts of disease pressures apply. In a warm, dry climate, there is little risk of the fungal diseases that preoccupy winemakers in cooler, damper regions, so organic practices can easily be adopted. On the other hand, by avoiding use of chemicals, producers can actually save money by growing grapes organically, just as long as they can maintain the health and yield of their crop.

Did you know?

Winegrowers of the premium-quality south New Zealand region of Central Otago are considering declaring their whole region organic. By the time you read this, it may have already happened.

A variant on organic practices is Biodynamics, which could be described as a more extreme and demanding version of organics. No synthetic products are allowed, and much emphasis is placed on composting to keep the plants in top condition. Producers also apply homeopathic doses of a range of Biodynamic preparations to the vines. Applications of these specially 'dynamized' preparations are timed to coincide with the movements of the moon and planets, using techniques pioneered in the 1920s by Austrian philosopher, Rudolf Steiner. Despite being dubbed 'voodoo viticulture' by some, the unconventional practices of Biodynamics are lent credibility by the growing band of opinion-forming winemakers adopting the techniques in their vineyards and producing wines of excellent quality.

Sustainable wine buying

Increasingly, we expect all our purchases to be produced in a sustainable manner. In wine, as elsewhere, this is currently a very loosely defined term, though attempts are being made to come up with meaningful definitions that apply specifically to wine. You might think that wine, being an agricultural product, is naturally sustainable, but once you take account of fuel, electricity, water and agrochemical usage, plus producing and transporting heavy glass bottles containing relatively little liquid halfway around the world, it becomes clear that there are significant environmental costs of producing wine. The wine business is busy trying to come up with standard ways to count the carbon cost of wine in the same way as this is being done for other products. At the time of writing, this is still mired in confusion.

> **Did you know?**
> An Italian study from the University of Palermo found that 50 per cent of the environmental pressure of a wine was its glass bottle.

Meanwhile, if you want to be more sustainable in your wine buying, think first about the weight of the bottle you are buying. Winemakers put their wine in heavy bottles (which are, incidentally, often not recyclable) to indicate quality. You can shop more sustainably by refusing to be fooled by this marketing ruse. Before too long, heavy bottles will be probably be seen not as a symbol of quality, but of environmental slackness on the part of the wine producer.

Another development you will see is that more wine is being transported in bulk and bottled where it is sold, thus reducing the weight of glass that is transported. Don't discount alternative packaging to glass. Retailers are increasingly trying out new, more environmentally-friendly packaging formats, and not just for the cheapest wines.

Try this

Your friends may think this curious behaviour, but try weighing your empty wine bottles. An average bottle will weigh about 500 grams, but some weigh in at over 1,500 grams!

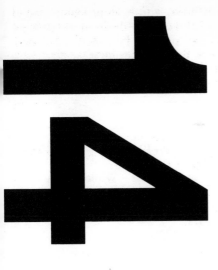

14

storing wine

In this chapter you will learn:
- the best (and worst) conditions for storing wine at home
- how long wine should be stored
- how best to preserve wine once it has been opened.

If you've got this far in this book, you have probably started buying more wine than you are going to drink in the next 24 hours. So now you need to make sure you look after it to ensure it is in good condition when you want to drink it.

Why store wine?

There are a few good reasons:

- **Give yourself more choice** – It's nice to have a choice of things to drink at home.
- **Drink wines when they are at their best** – While most wine is made to be drunk young, there are plenty of wines that will evolve and improve over time, whether it is in the next six months or the next few years.
- **Save money** – Most wine that is sold is young wine, from the most recent vintages. Anything older has necessarily had to be stored by someone else, so the price of this will be built into the cost of the wine. If you have the space to store wine yourself, you might as well do so, especially if you want to have access to the wines you like whenever you want.
- **Take control** – See for yourself how a wine you like evolves over time.
- **Access wines in short supply** – Sometimes the only way to get hold of wines that are in short supply or great demand (or both) is to buy them before they have even been bottled. In this case, you'll probably have to buy at least a case of 12 bottles, in which case you'll have to think about storing it.

How do you know whether a wine should be stored before opening or not?

It's a difficult question. Sometimes you will get notes on the bottle to guide you, and sometimes the person selling the wine will be helpful enough to have provided a guide to when the wine is to be drunk. Beyond this, you can read up on former vintages of the wine (or better still, try to taste them) to get an idea of how the wine might age.

But remember, drinking guidelines are only guidelines, not fixed rules. There are two things to remember: the first is that nobody really knows how a wine will age; it's an educated guess, at best. Second, the only person who knows how you like your wine is you. Some people love the taste of old wine, but for most of us, young wine is just as enjoyable, especially now that new winemaking techniques mean that most wines are drinkable right away. A senior member of the British wine trade confided to me recently that he'd never been disappointed by opening a bottle too early, but had frequently been disappointed by wine he felt he'd left too long in his cellar.

A good guide, if you have a few bottles of a wine, is to consider whether or not you like the wine now. If it tastes really good, the chances are it's good to drink. If, however, you feel there is some element of imbalance in the wine, especially tannins (including oak tannins in white wines), this is an indication you might want to wait a while for the wine to become better integrated.

Storing bottled wine

The best way to store wine is in a cool, dark, damp cellar. If you are lucky enough to have one, read no further (just make sure you can keep a track of what wine you have if the labels fall off). But for most of us, a proper cellar is not an option. So what can you do to provide your wine with the best living conditions to survive until you open the bottle?

There are several home cellar alternatives to a conventional cellar, including spiral underground cellars and wine fridges. The most important consideration is the range of temperatures to which your wine is exposed. You should try to keep the temperature as constant as possible.

Here are the things you should try to avoid:

- extremes of temperature fluctuation
- high temperatures
- vibration
- bright light.

Wine should be stored lying down to stop the cork from drying out. If you notice wine seeping out of a bottle, it has probably been exposed to heat that has caused the cork to expand and push out of the bottle (you might notice this in wine stored in shops with no air conditioning during particularly hot weather).

A small amount of heat (even extreme heat), or vibration (from a plane or car journey) is unlikely to do a wine much harm. But prolonged exposure to heat will mean that wine will age faster than if it is stored in a cooler place.

Professional storage options

This is a good option if you have a significant quantity of wine that you know you won't be opening for a while. You pay an amount per case per year, and you'll usually have to give a little notice to get the wine out.

Can you store wine sealed with a closure other than a cork?

Yes. An increasing number of fine wines are sealed with screwcap closures and the evidence suggests that the wines age extremely well sealed in this way. Plastic corks have been less successful for ageing wines, and these tend to be used for wines that are to be drunk within the first year or two of bottling.

Storing an opened bottle

Soon after you open a bottle of wine it will start to deteriorate. This is due to the presence of oxygen. Beneficial in small amounts to 'fast-age' a wine, oxygen will soon start to oxidize a wine, leaving it flat and dull (see Chapter 13 for how to tell if a wine is oxidized).

There is an astonishing range of products on sale to re-seal wine, but there are only two basic techniques to try to preserve an open bottle of wine. The first is to stop further oxygen entering the bottle. There are many products on sale to do this, but as long as there is oxygen in the bottle, it will destroy the remaining wine in the same way as if you re-sealed it with the original cork.

The second, and far preferable, option to preserve wine is to try to remove as much of the oxygen in the bottle as possible. This can be achieved by using a vacuum pump, or by displacing the oxygen with other, inert gases. Both are more effective than merely resealing the bottle and will enable you to keep your wine fresher for longer.

Vacuum pumps literally suck the oxygen out of the wine. They have the advantage that they are cheap and easy to use, and additional stoppers can be purchased separately. The main disadvantage of these is that when the oxygen is removed some of the more volatile aromas of the wine are also sucked out. Newer versions of these pumps have indicators, or make clicking sounds, so that you know when to stop pumping the vacuum, which mitigates this problem to some extent.

Spraying inert gas into the wine is an option that works well to preserve the most delicate aromas and flavours in wine and is probably the best option. The only disadvantages of this are that it seems rather an imprecise business to know how much gas to spray in, and also there is no warning when the bottle (which feels empty from the start) is about to run out.

An alternative solution for storing wine is to keep an empty half bottle to hand and to store your opened wine in this. If you know in advance that you only want to drink half a bottle, you can keep the wine even fresher by pouring half of it into a half bottle right after opening it and sealing it with a cork.

taking it further

Courses, wine clubs and tastings

Where there are wine enthusiasts, there are wine clubs and tasting groups. For group wine education, there are numerous individuals offering courses. Look up the Association of Wine Educators (**www.wineeducators.com**) to find someone in your area. For a formal approach, leading to professional wine exams (although they are open to anyone), contact the Wine and Spirit Education Trust (**www.wset.co.uk**), which has courses throughout the world. Auctioneers Sotheby's and Christie's offer fine wine courses. Many wine merchants offer one-off tastings and courses, or some will sell you tastings that you can organize yourself at home. You can look out for tastings in your area at **www.localwineevents.com/**.

General information

There is a wealth of free information available from regional wine promotion bodies and commercial organizations on the internet. Here you can find out more details about individual producers, grape varieties and regional specialities for each country. Below are some of the main sources of information.

Wikipedia is a good starting point for general country and regional information: **www.wikipedia.org/**. To filter unwanted information, try **www.ablegrape.com/**, a wine-only search engine.

France

Bordeaux – www.vins-bordeaux.fr/
Champagne – www.champagne.fr/
Alsace – www.vinsalsace.com/
Burgundy – www.burgundy-wines.fr/
Rhône – www.vins-rhone.com/
Loire Valley – www.loirevalleywine.com/
Languedoc-Roussillon – www.languedoc-wines.com/,
  www.vinsduroussillon.com/

Italy

www.italianmade.com/wines/home.cfm
Piedmont – www.piedmontwines.net/
Tuscany – www.wine-toscana.com/

Spain

www.winesfromspain.com/
Rioja – www.riojawine.com/
Ribera del Duero – www.riberadelduero.es/

Portugal

www.portugalinbusiness.com/

Germany

www.winesofgermany.co.uk/
www.germanwineestates.com/

Austria

www.winesfromaustria.com/

England

www.englishwineproducers.com/

USA

www.wineinstitute.org/
www.california-wine.org/
www.oregonwine.org/
www.washingtonwine.org/
www.newyorkwines.org/

Australia

www.wineaustralia.com/

New Zealand

www.nzwine.com/

Chile

www.winesofchile.org/

Argentina

www.winesofargentina.org/

South Africa

www.wosa.co.za/

Uruguay

www.winesofuruguay.com/

Magazines and news sources

Many magazines issue newsletters and email alerts that you can sign up for, usually free of charge.

Decanter – www.decanter.com/ UK-based monthly magazine.

Wine Spectator – www.winespectator.com/ The leading US wine magazine.

The World of Fine Wine – www.finewinemag.com/ Quarterly heavyweight magazine, with in-depth coverage of the top end of the wine market.

The Wine Advocate – www.erobertparker.com/ Tasting-led subscription newsletter by Robert Parker and team.

Wine Enthusiast – www.winemag.com/ Influential and established US-based monthly covering wine, spirits and lifestyle.

Quarterly Review of Wines – www.qrw.com/ America's oldest quarterly about wine.

Food & Wine magazine – www.foodandwine.com/ Lively American magazine with popular website.

Wine & Spirit – www.wine-spirit.com/ UK magazine for consumers and wine trade professionals.

Wine & Spirits – www.wineandspiritsmagazine.com/ US monthly.

Individual websites

www.jancisrobinson.com/ Subscription-based website from leading wine authority, Jancis Robinson, with some free content.

www.erobertparker.com/ The subscription website of the USA's most influential palate, Robert Parker.

www.wine-pages.com/ Free site, and one of the earliest wine-dedicated websites, by Tom Cannavan.

www.wineanorak.com/ Despite the title, an eminently approachable, free site from self-styled geek, Jamie Goode.

Vintage information

Magazine websites are a useful reference, especially Robert Parker and *Decanter*. If you start to sign up for newsletters from wine merchants, you will soon be receiving current vintage reports from the world's fine wine regions.

Wine price checker

www.wine-searcher.com/

Comprehensive site enabling searches by market, converted to your currency of choice.

Wine glasses

Too many choices to list here, but see **www.riedel.com/** for the most comprehensive range of glasses suitable for wine.

Ethical and green wine consumption

Fairtrade – **www.fairtrade.org.uk/**

Organics – Becoming increasingly mainstream, there are now organic wines to match wines at any quality level. There are many organic bodies, even within single countries, that monitor the production of organic goods. In the UK, the most important body for organic agriculture is the Soil Association, **www.soilassociation.org/**. There is plenty written about organic wines in the regular press. For a specialist view, take a look at **www.organicwinejournal.com/**, a US site dedicated to organic wines.

Biodynamics – Demeter, **www.demeter.net/**, is the certifying body of Biodynamics across the world. The site explains the basics of Biodynamics. Another good resource is **www.biodynamics.com/**. In France, there are two main organizations for international winemakers practising

Biodynamics: the larger of the two is Renaissance des Appellations – **www.biodynamy.com/**; the other is Biodyvin – **www.biodyvin.com/**. In Australia, **www.biodynamics.net.au/**, Red, White and Green is a website dedicated to Biodynamics, written by journalist, Max Allen.

Sustainable winegrowing

There are sustainable initiatives springing up all over the world, but it can be hard to keep track of the different criteria of each. Below are some of the most prominent.

USA

California Sustainable Winegrowing Alliance –
www.sustainablewinegrowing.org/
Oregon Tilth – **www.tilth.org/**
Low Input Viticulture and Enology (Oregon) –
www.liveinc.org/

South Africa

Integrated Production of Wine – **www.ipw.co.za/**
Biodiversity and Wine Initiative – **www.bwi.co.za/**

Australia

National Association for Sustainable Agriculture Australia –
www.nasaa.com.au/

New Zealand

Sustainable Winegrowing New Zealand –
www.nzwine.com/swnz/

Responsible consumption

Alcohol in Moderation – **www.aim-digest.com/** A useful site, giving information about the health effects of wine consumption and responsible drinking.

More from this author

www.beverleyblanning.com

Reference books

Broadbent, M. (2007) *Michael Broadbent's Pocket Vintage Wine Companion*, London: Pavilion Books. Long-established, compact guide that is of particular interest for Broadbent's experienced views on older vintages and the performance of different wine regions over time.

Jefford, A. (2002) *The New France*, Great Britain: Mitchell Beazley. The mellifluous prose and keen insight of Andrew Jefford make compelling reading for anyone interested in gaining a better understanding of French wines.

Johnson, H. (2008) *Pocket Wine Book,* Great Britain: Mitchell Beazley. The original and still the best annual pocket guide to wines, which manages to cram an improbable amount of information within its slim covers.

Johnson, H. and Robinson, J. (2007) *The World Atlas of Wine*, Great Britain: Mitchell Beazley. Highly informative atlas of all the most important wine-producing places on earth.

Robinson, J. (ed) (2006) *The Oxford Companion to Wine*, USA: Oxford University Press. The definitive guide for anyone serious about wine, with the answer to any wine question you can think of.

Robinson, J. (1996) *Jancis Robinson's Guide to Wine Grapes,* Great Britain: Oxford University Press. Pocket guide that tells you all you need to know about grapes.

Saunderson, P. (2004) *Wine Label Language*, New Zealand: Firefly. A single reference to explain labelling language and grape varieties by region and sub-region.

Stevenson, T. (ed) *Wine Report 2009,* Great Britain: Dorling Kindersley. Annual guide written by regional experts, providing up-to-date news and views. Aimed at the informed reader, it nevertheless contains plenty of accessible and opinionated comment for the novice wine drinker.

Williamson, P. & Moore, D. (2007) *Wine behind the Label*, Great Britain: BTL Publishing. A much-acclaimed book that details top wineries around the world. Includes contact details for all wineries listed.

glossary

General glossary

Appellation – Geographical indication that specifies where grapes for a wine were grown. Can be large or very small.

Bâtonnage – A French word meaning 'lees stirring', a process used to add richness and flavour to white wines.

Botrytis – A form of rot affecting grapes. It can be beneficial (see noble rot, below) or highly damaging, when it is more usually known as grey rot.

Chaptalization – Common practice of adding sugar to grape must prior to fermentation to increase the alcoholic strength of a wine.

Finish/length – The impression a wine leaves in the mouth after it has been spat or swallowed.

Ice wine – Rare and expensive wine made from grapes that are left for months after harvest to freeze on the vine and crushed when frozen, giving more concentrated sweetness.

Malolactic fermentation – A naturally occurring process that can be suppressed or encouraged during winemaking after the alcoholic fermentation has taken place. Malolactic fermentation transforms sharp malic acid into softer, lactic acid. It takes place for virtually all red wines and many (but by no means all) white wines.

Must – Deriving from crushed grapes, this is the pre-fermented grape matter. It includes pulp, skins and seeds of the grapes.

New world – Commonly used term for non-European wine-producing countries – even if wine production in such places has centuries of history. New world countries include the USA, Australia, New Zealand, South Africa and the countries of Central and South America.

Noble rot – A benevolent form of rot where the fungus, *Botrytis cinerea* (often referred to simply as botrytis), attacks healthy grapes without harmfully penetrating their skins. A cycle of humidity followed by dry, warm weather at the end of the ripening season can lead to this desirable infection. The grapes become shrivelled and look mouldy and black, but stay healthy so long as the berries remain intact. Noble rot concentrates the flavours and aromas in grapes to produce some of the world's finest sweet wines, which are also referred to as botrytized wines.

Old world – Commonly used term for the traditional wine-producing nations of Europe.

Varietal – Used interchangeably with 'variety' to denote a particular cultivar of the *Vitis vinifera* vine species from which almost all wine is made. Varietal wine is wine made from a single grape variety, rather than a blend.

French glossary

Blanc – White.

Blanc de blancs – White wine made from white grapes – so named to distinguish it from blanc de noirs (below).

Blanc de noirs – White wine made from black grapes.

Cave – Cellar.

Château – Literally, castle, but more usually a name for a property (more common in Bordeaux than elsewhere).

Clos – Enclosed vineyard.

Côte – Slope.

Cru – Literally, growth, usually a specific site or area for growing grapes.

Cuvée – Blend.

Domaine – Domain or estate.

Dosage – Mixture of sugar and wine used to sweeten Champagne at the final stage in its production.

Doux – Sweet.

Lieu-dit – Specified vineyard site.

Méthode traditionelle – Traditional method (used in the context of making sparkling wine in the same way as in Champagne).

Millésime – Vintage.

Mis en bouteille – Bottled.

Pourriture noble – Noble rot (see above).

Récolte – Harvest.

Rouge – Red.

Sec – Dry.

Sélection de Grains Nobles (SGN) – Term for botrytized sweet wine in Alsace.

Vendange(s) Tardive(s) – Late harvest.

Vieilles vignes – Old vines.

Vigneron – Vine grower and winemaker.

Vignoble – Vineyard.

Viticulteur – Vine grower.

German glossary

Auslese – Usually sweet wine made from very late-harvest grapes.

Beerenauslese – Sweet wine (generally sweeter than Auslese) made from late-harvested berries, a proportion of which will have been affected by noble rot. Sometimes abbreviated to BA.

Bereich – District or region.

Edelfaüle – Noble rot (see above).

Einzellage – Individual site or vineyard.

Eiswein – Ice wine (see above).

Erzeugerabfüllung/Gutsabfüllung – Estate bottled.

Erstes Gewächs – Quality designation of the Rheingau, meaning 'first growths', with the same status as Grosses Gewächs (below).

Grosses Gewächs – Quality designation, meaning 'great growths'.

Gutswein – Estate wine.

Halbtrocken/Feinherb – Medium-dry.

Mit Prädikat – With special attributes.

Sekt – German sparkling wine.

Spätburgunder – Pinot Noir.

Spätlese – Late harvest.

Trocken – Dry.

Trockenbeerenauslese – Very rich, sweet wine made from late-harvested grapes affected by noble rot (see above). Sometimes abbreviated to TBA.

Weingut – Wine estate.

Spanish glossary

Blanco – White.

Bodega – Winery.

Cava – Sparkling wine made in the traditional method, as in Champagne.

Cosecha – Vintage.

Crianza – Wine aged for two or more years after the harvest, of which six months in oak.

Dulce – Sweet.

Embotellado – Bottled.

Gran reserva – Wine aged for five or more years, of which two in oak and three in bottle.

Joven – Young, a wine with no ageing.

Reserva – Wine aged for three or more years after the harvest, of which one in oak and one in bottle.

Rosado – Rosé.

Seco – Dry.

Tinto – Red.

Vendimia – Vintage.

Viejo (or muy viejo) – Old (or very old).

Viña/viñedo – Vineyard.

Italian glossary

Abbocato – Lightly sweet.

Annata – Vintage.

Amabile – Medium sweet.

Azienda agricola – Winegorowing estate.

Classico – Quality indication, denoting the region the grapes were grown.

Consorzio – Local growers' association.

Dolce – Sweet.

Fattoria – Farm, winegrowing estate.

Frizzante – Lightly sparkling.

Imbottigliato – Bottled.

Metodo classico/tradizionale – Sparkling wine made in the traditional method, as in Champagne.

Passito – Made from dried grapes.

Rosato – Rosé.

Rosso – Red.

Secco – Dry.

Spumante – Sparkling.

Tenuta – Vineyard estate.

Vendemmia – Vintage.

Vigna/vigneto – Vineyard.

Vin santo – Style of dried grape wine, usually sweet.

Chapter 03

'Climate and Terroir: Impacts of Climate Variability and Change on Wine', Jones, G.V. (2006) in *Fine Wine and Terroir – The Geoscience Perspective*.

Macqueen, R. W., and Meinert, L. D., (eds.), *Geoscience, Canada* Reprint Series Number 9, Geological Association of Canada, St. John's, Newfoundland, 247 pp.

Chapter 06

'Sense and Sense-ability; the key to broadening the wine market? The human hardware and software that drives sensation and perception.' Presentation by Dr. Charles J. Wysocki, given at the Institute of Masters of Wine Symposium, Napa, 30 June 2006.

'Exploring the potentials of human olfaction: an interview with Alan R. Hirsch, MD, FACP' Russ Mason, MS: *Alternative & Complementary Therapies*, June 2005, Vol 11, (3), p. 135.

'Wine & Song: The Effect of Background Music on the Taste of Wine', Dr Adrian C. North, Professor of Psychology, School of Life Sciences, Heriot Watt University, Edinburgh EH14 4AS.

North, A. C., Hargreaves, D. J., and McKendrick, J. (1997), 'In-store music affects product choice', *Nature*, 390, 132.

index

Note: Page numbers in bold are for glossary entries, e.g.: blanc de noirs **227**
Page ranges followed by 'passim' mean there is at least one mention of the topic
on every page in the sequence, e.g. France, wine styles 102–22*passim*

From Advanced Sudoku to Zulu, you'll find everything you need in the **teach yourself** range, in books, on CD and on DVD.

Visit **www.teachyourself.co.uk** for more details.

Advanced Sudoku and Kakuro
Afrikaans
Alexander Technique
Algebra
Ancient Greek
Applied Psychology
Arabic
Arabic Conversation
Aromatherapy
Art History
Astrology
Astronomy
AutoCAD 2004
AutoCAD 2007
Ayurveda
Baby Massage and Yoga
Baby Signing
Baby Sleep
Bach Flower Remedies
Backgammon
Ballroom Dancing
Basic Accounting
Basic Computer Skills
Basic Mathematics
Beauty
Beekeeping
Beginner's Arabic Script
Beginner's Chinese Script
Beginner's Dutch

Beginner's French
Beginner's German
Beginner's Greek
Beginner's Greek Script
Beginner's Hindi
Beginner's Hindi Script
Beginner's Italian
Beginner's Japanese
Beginner's Japanese Script
Beginner's Latin
Beginner's Mandarin Chinese
Beginner's Portuguese
Beginner's Russian
Beginner's Russian Script
Beginner's Spanish
Beginner's Turkish
Beginner's Urdu Script
Bengali
Better Bridge
Better Chess
Better Driving
Better Handwriting
Biblical Hebrew
Biology
Birdwatching
Blogging
Body Language
Book Keeping
Brazilian Portuguese

Bridge
British Citizenship Test, The
British Empire, The
British Monarchy from Henry VIII, The
Buddhism
Bulgarian
Bulgarian Conversation
Business French
Business Plans
Business Spanish
Business Studies
C++
Calculus
Calligraphy
Cantonese
Caravanning
Car Buying and Maintenance
Card Games
Catalan
Chess
Chi Kung
Chinese Medicine
Christianity
Classical Music
Coaching
Cold War, The
Collecting
Computing for the Over 50s
Consulting
Copywriting
Correct English
Counselling
Creative Writing
Cricket
Croatian
Crystal Healing
CVs
Czech
Danish
Decluttering
Desktop Publishing
Detox
Digital Home Movie Making
Digital Photography
Dog Training

Drawing
Dream Interpretation
Dutch
Dutch Conversation
Dutch Dictionary
Dutch Grammar
Eastern Philosophy
Electronics
English as a Foreign Language
English Grammar
English Grammar as a Foreign Language
Entrepreneurship
Estonian
Ethics
Excel 2003
Feng Shui
Film Making
Film Studies
Finance for Non-Financial Managers
Finnish
First World War, The
Fitness
Flash 8
Flash MX
Flexible Working
Flirting
Flower Arranging
Franchising
French
French Conversation
French Dictionary
French for Homebuyers
French Grammar
French Phrasebook
French Starter Kit
French Verbs
French Vocabulary
Freud
Gaelic
Gaelic Conversation
Gaelic Dictionary
Gardening
Genetics
Geology

Lithuanian
Magic
Mahjong
Malay
Managing Stress
Managing Your Own Career
Mandarin Chinese
Mandarin Chinese Conversation
Marketing
Marx
Massage
Mathematics
Meditation
Middle East Since 1945, The
Modern China
Modern Hebrew
Modern Persian
Mosaics
Music Theory
Mussolini's Italy
Nazi Germany
Negotiating
Nepali
New Testament Greek
NLP
Norwegian
Norwegian Conversation
Old English
One-Day French
One-Day French – the DVD
One-Day German
One-Day Greek
One-Day Italian
One-Day Polish
One-Day Portuguese
One-Day Spanish
One-Day Spanish – the DVD
One-Day Turkish
Origami
Owning a Cat
Owning a Horse
Panjabi
PC Networking for Small
  Businesses
Personal Safety and Self
  Defence

Philosophy
Philosophy of Mind
Philosophy of Religion
Phone French
Phone German
Phone Italian
Phone Japanese
Phone Mandarin Chinese
Phone Spanish
Photography
Photoshop
PHP with MySQL
Physics
Piano
Pilates
Planning Your Wedding
Polish
Polish Conversation
Politics
Portuguese
Portuguese Conversation
Portuguese for Homebuyers
Portuguese Grammar
Portuguese Phrasebook
Postmodernism
Pottery
PowerPoint 2003
PR
Project Management
Psychology
Quick Fix French Grammar
Quick Fix German Grammar
Quick Fix Italian Grammar
Quick Fix Spanish Grammar
Quick Fix: Access 2002
Quick Fix: Excel 2000
Quick Fix: Excel 2002
Quick Fix: HTML
Quick Fix: Windows XP
Quick Fix: Word
Quilting
Recruitment
Reflexology
Reiki
Relaxation
Retaining Staff

Romanian
Running Your Own Business
Russian
Russian Conversation
Russian Grammar
Sage Line 50
Sanskrit
Screenwriting
Second World War, The
Serbian
Setting Up a Small Business
Shorthand Pitman 2000
Sikhism
Singing
Slovene
Small Business Accounting
Small Business Health Check
Songwriting
Spanish
Spanish Conversation
Spanish Dictionary
Spanish for Homebuyers
Spanish Grammar
Spanish Phrasebook
Spanish Starter Kit
Spanish Verbs
Spanish Vocabulary
Speaking On Special Occasions
Speed Reading
Stalin's Russia
Stand Up Comedy
Statistics
Stop Smoking
Sudoku
Swahili
Swahili Dictionary
Swedish
Swedish Conversation
Tagalog
Tai Chi
Tantric Sex
Tap Dancing
Teaching English as a Foreign
   Language
Teams & Team Working
Thai

Thai Conversation
Theatre
Time Management
Tracing Your Family History
Training
Travel Writing
Trigonometry
Turkish
Turkish Conversation
Twentieth Century USA
Typing
Ukrainian
Understanding Tax for Small
   Businesses
Understanding Terrorism
Urdu
Vietnamese
Visual Basic
Volcanoes, Earthquakes and
   Tsunamis
Watercolour Painting
Weight Control through Diet &
   Exercise
Welsh
Welsh Conversation
Welsh Dictionary
Welsh Grammar
Wills & Probate
Windows XP
Wine Tasting
Winning at Job Interviews
Word 2003
World Faiths
Writing Crime Fiction
Writing for Children
Writing for Magazines
Writing a Novel
Writing a Play
Writing Poetry
Xhosa
Yiddish
Yoga
Your Wedding
Zen
Zulu